WOMEN AND THE AMERICAN ECONOMY

D1016174

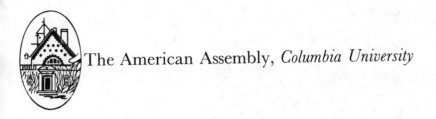 The American Assembly, *Columbia University*

WOMEN AND
THE AMERICAN
ECONOMY
A LOOK TO THE 1980s

Prentice-Hall, Inc., *Englewood Cliffs, New Jersey*

A SPECTRUM BOOK

Library of Congress Cataloging in Publication Data
Main entry under title:

Women and the American economy.

(A Spectrum Book)
At head of title: The American Assembly, Columbia
University.

Background papers for the American Assembly which met
in the fall of 1975 at Arden House, Harriman, N.Y.

Includes index.

1.-Women in business—Addresses, essays, lectures.
2.-Women—Employment—United States—Addresses,
essays, lectures.   3.-Discrimination in employment—
Addresses, essays, lectures.   4.-Women—United States—
Social conditions—Addresses, essays, lectures.
I. American Assembly.

HQ1381.W64   331.4'0973   76-4105
ISBN 0-13-962324-8
ISBN 0-13-962316-7 pbk.

© 1976 by the American Assembly, Columbia University, under International and Pan-American Copyright Conventions. All rights reserved. No part of this book may be reproduced in any form or by any means without permission in writing from the publisher. Printed in the United States of America.

10 9 8 7 6 5 4 3 2 1

PRENTICE-HALL INTERNATIONAL, INC. (*London*)
PRENTICE-HALL OF AUSTRALIA PTY., LTD. (*Sydney*)
PRENTICE-HALL OF CANADA, LTD. (*Toronto*)
PRENTICE-HALL OF INDIA PRIVATE LIMITED (*New Delhi*)
PRENTICE-HALL OF JAPAN, INC. (*Tokyo*)
PRENTICE-HALL OF SOUTHEAST ASIA PTE., LTD. (*Singapore*)

Table of Contents

Preface

For American women, changes in the world of work since World War II have been profound and are irreversible. Even so, the women's revolution of rising expectations is still going on—and is in fact only in its youth.

This opinion was made plain by a large majority of the participants in The American Assembly, at Arden House, Harriman, New York, in the fall of 1975, on *Women and the American Economy*. Their final statement (not included here but available in a pamphlet from The American Assembly) said that "although their work activity has grown dramatically, the value assigned to women's market work remains well below that of men." There is much to be done. Low wages, restriction of women to service and low-status occupations, limitations on job training, constraints on entry to high-level jobs: these and other problems combine to maintain a wide gap between the present role of women and their full and free participation in the economy. Institutional changes are "critical if society is to gain the full measure of women's potential, acquired skills and competence," the Assembly felt.

This book reviews in short compass the history of women at work in America, outlines and analyzes current issues, and on the basis of past and present looks to some of the major questions which will need answering in the next decade. It was planned and edited by Juanita M. Kreps, Vice President and Professor of Economics at Duke University, as advance reading for the Arden House Assembly. But it goes beyond the relatively narrow scope of *ad hoc* background reading. The breadth of the discussion in these pages makes it clear that the lives of all of us—men and children included—will be influenced by this quiet revolution. "The faster is the pace of progress in removing all discriminatory attitudes and behavior toward women, the greater will be the benefits to [all of] society." The volume is therefore of more than academic interest and should have appeal for the general reader.

The opinions on these pages belong to the writers themselves and not to The American Assembly, a nonpartisan public affairs forum, which takes no official position. Nor is The Ford Foundation, which generously underwrote this entire Forty-ninth American Assembly program, to be associated with any of the views herein.

Clifford C. Nelson
President
The American Assembly

WOMEN AND THE AMERICAN ECONOMY

Juanita M. Kreps

Introduction

At the beginning of this last quarter-century, women make up about forty percent of the nation's labor force. They are going to school longer, marrying later, having fewer children, and living decades beyond the lifespan of their grandmothers. The forces that shaped these changes in women's lives—industrialization, urbanization, higher levels of learning and a consequent rise in living standards—have left their imprint on the worklives and expectations of men as well, and on the economic potential of the nation.

The process through which these major social transformations changed aspirations and led society to accept women in a wider range of roles has been slow and uneven. From early in the century when a double standard endorsed hard physical labor for black and immigrant women but held that for white middle-class women to want careers seemed "a violation of nature," William Chafe shows that the pace of change slowed after the initial promise of the suffragette movement, accelerated with the Second World War, and after a quiet postwar era saw its most significant developments during the past decade. A constellation of social and economic forces in the late 1960s (sharply declining birthrates, later marriages, higher labor force activity among married women, careerism among those in college) gave support to

JUANITA M. KREPS *is Vice President and James B. Duke Professor of Economics at Duke University. In addition to leading textbooks in economics she has written extensively in the areas of labor and manpower. Dr. Kreps is a director of the New York Stock Exchange, J. C. Penney Co., Western Electric, R. J. Reynolds Industries, and the North Carolina National Bank. Her most recent book is* Sex in the Market Place.

the drive for sex equality that originated with the Civil Rights movement.

The question of equality is now being posed in the context of an economic environment that is noticeably different from that of a decade ago. It is important to ask whether the economy's potential will be achieved, thereby allowing both men and women maximum career opportunity and some freedom of choice as to how they will spend their lives. As Nancy Barrett warns, a continuation of today's high level of unemployment would threaten such opportunity and would be particularly discouraging to women. The conflict between seniority practice and the goals of affirmative action programs is further emphasized by Phyllis Wallace, who describes the measures through which equal opportunity is now mandated.

Laws specifying equal access to educational opportunity and to jobs reflect important changes in the roles of women. The traditional division of work into market jobs for men and nonmarket for women has been eroded by changes in the nature of work in both places: in the market, from heavy manual labor to white-collar services; and in the home, from time-consuming family production to time-saving appliances and the purchase of goods prepared elsewhere. The availability of market jobs thought appropriate for women, along with improved household technology and smaller families, induced women to enter the labor force in numbers that challenged the earlier pattern of work allocation. Authors Taeuber and Sweet show that secular movements toward higher levels of education and a gradual decline in age at first marriage during the first half of the twentieth century combined to bring added impetus to workforce participation. Finally, declining mortality and fertility rates, and a closer spacing of births, greatly affected family formation and the ability of women to spend long periods in the labor force.

But the range of jobs held by women has tended to be quite narrow. Stereotyping of work which formerly separated the sexes into market and nonmarket categories now tends to divide the labor market into men's jobs and women's jobs. Analyzing separate pools of labor in a large private firm, Harris Schrank and John Riley find that these pools are differentiated by sex composition, with men occupying the professional and managerial positions, women the clerical and secretarial. Positions in the women's pool, even when at the peak level for that group, rank only on a par with lower-middle status male pools. The lack of male movement into female pools and the lower status of the latter produce a caste notion of inferior status for female workers.

Recent reduction in the degree of sex segregation of job pools leads the authors to be optimistic about the eventual breakdown of the caste system. Some of the consequences of both the high proportions of women in market work and the gradual improvements in levels of jobs open to women are now being studied. Is greater financial independence of women one of the factors that explains rising divorce rates? Probably, Kristin Moore and Isabel Sawhill conclude, since "empty-shell" marriages are likely to decline as women find alternatives to support from husbands. On the other hand the same alternative allows the selection of partners to be more discriminating, which would increase family stability. How are the children of working parents affected? Again, the authors find the evidence inconclusive. Earlier studies indicating higher rates of delinquency and lower educational attainment do not appear to be relevant to families in which both parents earn moderately high incomes and are able to provide adequate child care. Indeed, later studies suggest that the influence of employed parents could be to raise the aspirations and educational levels of their children. How are husband-wife relationships influenced by women's change in role? The working wife probably gains bargaining strength, particularly in any debate on financial decisions, as she contributes a larger fraction of total family income.

Decisions as to how to share home work, however, appear to be made in the traditional manner. Working women seem to cut down on the amount of home work they do, but pass very little of it on to their husbands. When both husband and wife work, the net effect is to reduce the free time available to the family, particularly the wife, despite a long-run reduction in the length of the workweek, an increase in holidays and vacations, etc. For while it is generally true that growth in productivity and income results in the consumption of more leisure (as incomes rise, the family can afford more goods and services and more free time), leisure time does not grow when the family goes from one market worker to two. As Juanita Kreps and John Leaper point out, intrafamily decisions as to how best to allocate the adults' time between the market and the home have important implications for the size and composition of the labor force. And decisions as to how to apportion home work within the household have equally important meaning for the members of the family.

In appraising the gains that accrue to the family and to the society as a result of increased participation in market work it is necessary to impute a value to the home services and free time that are foregone. Since neither home work nor leisure carries a price tag, it is difficult to measure the net improvement in human welfare; the national product rises with additional paid work but does not fall to take into account loss of nonmarket services. But it is not the accounting discrepancy that gives rise to current discussions of attaching a dollar value to work done in the home. Rather, the proposal is offered as a means of providing the same status and financial independence to women who work at home as to persons in the labor force. Moreover, payment for home work and child care would vest the woman with her own schedule of benefits, such as Social Security, which could not be lost through divorce.

Although such payments have had little serious consideration, Martha Griffiths makes a strong appeal for measures that will assure more equitable treatment of women by financial institutions. She argues that much greater political participation by women and the passage of the Equal Rights Amendment are necessary to insure equal access to education, jobs, and credit. Somewhat more optimistic in her evaluation, Phyllis Wallace finds that legislation and particularly recent court decisions have added great impetus to equal opportunity by attempting to deal with employment discrimination on a comprehensive basis. But she notes that problems associated with high levels of unemployment may bring a backlash against women.

While agreeing that continued unemployment might result in negative attitudes toward women in market jobs, Nancy Barrett sees the possibility that slowed growth could also bring shorter workweeks and more part-time work, giving both men and women more time for leisure and home work. The environment may change, she reasons, and market work may become less important as a source of status: "If the 1980s mark an important period of transition in lifestyles—a transition toward greater conservation, less emphasis on large families, more equitable sharing of work—the gains to both sexes could be more significant than those of earlier decades."

The significance of the broad social forces that have changed the composition of the work force during the past half century is not yet fully appreciated. Nor is the revolution complete, for as William Chafe argues, "When people are raised with a set of attitudes and ideas as deeply embedded as those about sex roles, inequities rarely disappear quickly." Uncertainty as to economic circumstances in the decades ahead make it difficult to predict further transitions in the demand for labor, in incomes, and in the pace of industrial development. Future demographic movements are similarly subject to debate. Authors Taeuber and Sweet point out that "Social scientists looking forward to the 1980s, when cohort sizes will for the first time be falling sharply, differ in their judgment as to whether there will be a resurgence of familism with lowered age at marriage and increased childbearing." In appraising developments of the recent past, however, one can safely conclude that lifestyle changes for men and women have been quite profound; that the impact of such extraordinary beginnings will not be quickly dissipated.

William H. Chafe

1

Looking Backward

in Order to Look Forward:

Women, Work, and Social Values in America

In the midst of the Great Depression, the anthropologist Margaret Mead commented on the dilemma facing women who were interested in careers. A female had two choices, she noted. Either she proclaimed herself "a woman and therefore less an achieving individual, or an achieving individual and therefore less a woman." If she chose the first option, she increased her chances of being "a loved object, the kind of girl whom men will woo and boast of, toast and marry." But if she decided to pursue a career, she ran the risk of losing forever "as a woman, her chance for the kind of love she wants."

Mead's observation highlights the importance of considering social values in any discussion of women and work. Together with race and class, sex serves as a basic reference point around which our society is organized. It helps to determine how we are raised, which emotions we are taught to develop, what kind of power we exercise, how we relate to others, which jobs we can aspire to, and how we think of ourselves. Historically, social norms governing sex roles have divided the labor of life into

WILLIAM H. CHAFE *is Associate Professor of History at Duke University. Dr. Chafe is the author of* The American Woman: Her Changing Social, Political, and Economic Roles, 1920-1970 *and the forthcoming* Essays on Sex and Race in American Society. *He is also co-director of the Oral History Program at Duke University.*

male and female spheres. It is impossible, therefore, to assess the experience of women at work without considering the larger context of attitudes toward woman's "place." Behavior may influence attitudes, or attitudes may effect behavior, but like two parts of a puzzle, they bear an inextricable relationship to each other.

Historical Attitudes toward Woman's "Place"

Throughout American history, it has been customary to believe that women—especially white, middle-class women—could find happiness only through fulfilling their "biological destiny" and becoming good wives and mothers. "The home was the only field in which superior women might distinguish themselves," the historian Julia Cherry Spruill observed about life in the southern colonies. "Unmarried persons were regarded as pitiable encumberances." Within the family, a hierarchy was presumed to exist, with the man as the father and head, and women and children as his inferiors. Puritan New Englanders believed that the hierarchy reflected a divine pattern, with man's role in the home similar to God's role in the universe, but one did not have to be a Puritan to endorse the idea of patriarchy. "In truth," the nineteenth century southern sociologist George Fitzhugh observed, "woman, like children, has but one right and that is the right to protection. The right to protection involves the obligation to obey." If there was a model of perfection, it was the matron quoted in *The Spectator,* a colonial paper. "I am married," she wrote, "and I have no other concern but to please the man I love; he is the end of every care I have; if I dress, it is for him; if I read a poem, or a play, it is to qualify myself for a conversation agreeable to his taste; he is almost the end of my devotions."

Such sentiments sound familiar, of course, because they represent twentieth century norms as well. When Adlai Stevenson told the graduating women of Smith in 1955 that their task was to "influence man and boy" through the "humble role of housewife," he was essentially repeating *The Spectator's* eighteenth century injunction that women should "distinguish themselves as tender mothers and faithful wives rather than furious partisans." Since women's divinely ordained task was to support their husbands, care for their children, and provide a haven from the worries of the outside world, the idea that they might wish a ca-

reer seemed a violation of nature. As a woman's magazine observed in the 1930s,

> the office woman, no matter how successful, is a transplanted
> posy. . . . Just as a rose comes to its fullest beauty in its own appro-
> priate soil, so does a home woman come to her fairest blooming
> when her roots are stuck deep in the daily and hourly affairs of her
> own most dearly beloved.

Reality of Women's Work Experience Prior to 1900

Not surprisingly, the reality of women's experience in early
American history differed from the norm. In an overwhelmingly
agrarian society, there was little room for a leisure class or for a
rigid polarization of labor which would keep women confined
strictly to the home. Crops had to be planted and harvested, ani-
mals tended, clothes made, gardens cared for, and food prepared. Even in households with many servants, the woman frequently spent her day coordinating work activities, keeping
accounts, and planning how best to produce the goods required
to satisfy the food and clothing needs of various members of the
household. In most cases, of course, it was the woman herself
who spun the yarn, wove the cloth, kept the poultry, made the
butter and cheese, harvested the vegetables, and prepared the
food.

Other women engaged even more directly in the public economic life of the society. In a period when early death was a frequent occurrence, it was not unusual for a widow to find herself
in charge of a large plantation, a merchant business or a shop.
Although the socialization of women emphasized passivity rather
than assertiveness and genteel manners rather than business acu-
men, the average woman met such challenges without difficulty.
Women ran groceries and shops, practiced medicine, and served
as midwives, nurses, teachers, and printers; they also acted as
innkeepers, tavern hostesses, and laundresses. Whether through
their own initiative as business women or as a result of the un-
timely death of a husband, such individuals functioned effectively
in the world of commerce.

Nor were women excluded from the industrialism which swept
the nation during the nineteenth century. Young farm girls from
New Hampshire and Massachusetts flocked to Lowell in the
1830s and early 1840s to run the looms of the new textile mills

located there. Other women went to work in canning and to-
bacco factories. Although employment statistics for women in the
nineteenth century are somewhat unreliable, researchers have
found that in cities like Baltimore, a substantial part of the female population worked. By 1890, at least one million women
were employed in the nation's factories with many more working
in agricultural and domestic service.

Still, it is important to realize that the vast majority of gainfully
employed women were not from those groups covered by middle-class norms about woman's "place." Although the first factory women at Lowell were native and Protestant, they were soon
replaced by immigrants, especially when it became clear that the
mills were not providing the healthy environment initially adver-
tised by the mill owners. Indeed, there appears to have been a
double standard about women and employment just as there was
about women and morality. It was permissible—even desirable—
for black women and immigrant women to toil in fields and factories. Throughout the history of slavery, black women had been
expected to work as hard as men, hoeing in the fields as well as
providing domestic help. The same pattern continued after
emancipation, and in 1890, more than one million out of 2.7 million Negro girls and women were gainfully employed, half in agriculture and half as domestics. Similarly, hundreds of thousands
of immigrant women went into factories, did piecework in the
home, or served as domestics to help their families survive in the
new land. A Bureau of Labor study in 1887 found that among
17,000 women factory workers surveyed, 75 percent were of immigrant stock. Thus in ordinary circumstances, a clear line was
drawn between the "proper" white middle-class woman's life,
and that of the black, poor, or immigrant woman. The results
were dramatically apparent in the 1900 census which showed that
41 percent of all nonwhite women were employed while only 17
percent of white women worked—many of them immigrants.

The Middle-Class Woman and the Suffrage Movement

Nevertheless, white middle-class women were also affected
by the rising tide of industrialism. As urbanization increased in
the last part of the nineteenth century and factories began to
produce goods formerly made in the home, middle-class white
women became increasingly removed from the main stream eco-

nomic activities of life. Earlier, they had performed indispensable functions in an agricultural economy. Despite a division of labor according to sex, they worked in close association with others both outside the home and within it to produce the necessities of daily life. As people's places of work became geographically distant from their residence, however, a woman's participation in the economic activities of the family diminished steadily. Isolation increased and the separation of sexual spheres of activity became more pronounced. Although women continued to spend lengthy hours in homemaking tasks, they frequently did so without much contact with others. Ironically, with fewer children to care for because of a declining birth rate, and less direct involvement in activities outside the home, many middle-class women approached for the first time the social "ideal" of being primarily wives and mothers in a small nuclear family. As Alice Rossi and Bruno Bettelheim have pointed out, it was only in the twentieth century that childrearing and homemaking became a full time profession for women.

In the midst of these changes, a growing minority of middle-class women, especially those who were graduates of the new women's colleges, expressed dissatisfaction with what they saw as the wastefulness and narrowness of Victorian woman's role. In many instances, sending a girl to college was like letting the geni out of the bottle. Once having experienced the excitement of intellectual exploration and being treated as an equal in the world of knowledge, women graduates frequently were unwilling to resume the narrowly defined, homemaker role of their mothers. "I want to go and see something better than I have ever known," Cornelia Phillips, a young, well-educated woman, wrote in the nineteenth century. "I want to go, to take wings and fly and leave these sordid occupations. . . . I think sometimes it is cruel to cultivate tastes that are never to be gratified in this world." Jane Addams, another college graduate, experienced the same sense of frustration after finishing her education. Once her mind was opened, she wanted to help the world, only to be told that she should be satisfied with playing whist and serving tea. What was the purpose of education, she asked, if no work was to be provided for her.

Many among this first generation of college women pioneered in various business and professional occupations. By going to college, they had set themselves apart from their peers. Nor surprisingly, they were infused with a self-conscious sense of mission and a passionate commitment to improve the world. As a result, as many as 50 percent of female college graduates prior to 1900 chose to pursue a career. They became doctors, social workers, college professors, business women, lawyers, and architects. Spirited by an intense sense of purpose as well as camaraderie, they set a remarkable record of accomplishment in the face of overwhelming odds.

Other middle-class women, with or without college degrees, found an outlet for their energies in voluntary associations. Some joined the Women's Christian Temperance Union and campaigned for prohibition and the end of prostitution. Others worked in crusades for better educational facilities, playgrounds, and juvenile services for young children. The largest number took part in women's clubs. Initially devoted to cultural activities, these clubs became increasingly involved in such issues as child labor, pure food and drug legislation, conservation, and health reform. The General Federation of Women's Clubs, founded in 1889, had grown to more than a million members by the early twentieth century, and together with the WCTU and other similar associations provided the institutional voice through which middle-class women played an increasingly important role in political and social issues. Much of the reform ethos of the early twentieth century can be traced directly to the social welfare activities of career women such as Jane Addams, Julia Lathrop, and Alice Hamilton, and the increasing concern with the moral health of the society demonstrated by middle-class voluntary associations.

By the height of the Progressive era, career and club women had come to see woman's suffrage as a key vehicle for both advancing social welfare and eliminating the contradictions between men's status and women's status under the law. Suffrage had always been one of the key demands of women's rights advocates. The difference between the Seneca Falls conference of 1848 and the Progressive era was that the right to vote had become a more respectable and legitimate demand for middle-class reformers. To those concerned with social welfare issues, it promised a means for mobilizing half the population in support of child labor legislation and laws mandating better factory conditions. To those more interested in politics, the franchise appeared to be an ideal mechanism for purifying the political process by bringing to bear the moral sensibilities of women on the decisions of party leaders. And to those who were most concerned with altering the narrow definition of woman's "place," the vote seemed as good a place as any to start breaking down the barriers of sex discrimination. When the nineteenth amendment was ratified in 1920, many observers believed that it marked the beginning of a new era of sex equality.

The Experience of Women in the Labor Force from 1900 to 1940

Notwithstanding the high hopes of the suffragists, little change in women's status occurred during the two decades after 1920. In politics, initial fears of a female takeover faded once it became clear that women would not vote as a bloc. The threat of a continued feminist movement disintegrated as women activitists divided bitterly over the need for an Equal Rights Amendment. And within the economy itself, women remained a marginal, underpaid, and exploited underclass.

The most notable feature of female employment between 1900 and 1940 was how much remained the same. There were a number of changes, of course, especially in the types of work women did. In 1900 almost all women workers served as domestics, farm laborers, unskilled factory operatives, or teachers. By 1940 white-collar work and clerical jobs had increased substantially and the proportion of women engaged in nonmanual occupations had grown from 28.2 percent in 1910 to 45 percent in 1940. Also, there was an increase in the number of married women workers. In 1910 approximately 11 percent of all married women were employed while by 1940 the figure had climbed to approximately 15 percent, largely as a consequence of women taking jobs in order to help families survive during the Depression.

Overall, though, the picture of constancy was impressive. After an upsurge of female employment which coincided with the flood of foreign immigration at the turn of the century, the proportion of all women who held jobs remained stable, hovering around 25 percent from 1910 through 1940. Although World War I brought some new jobs for women, American involvement did not last long enough for the changes to be more than temporary. In 1940 as in 1900, the average woman worker was young, single, and poor. Even business and professional women showed little change. In 1920 approximately 12 percent of women workers were engaged in professional life. By 1940 the figure was 12.3 percent. The number of women medical doctors actually declined over time, and the proportion of women who were lawyers and architects remained constant (less than 3 percent). In no instance, it seems, did the suffrage movement or its consequences result in major shifts in women's economic status.

Throughout these years, what remains most striking is how thoroughly the traditional attitudes toward woman's "place" infused the treatment of women in the work force. To begin with, almost all employed women worked in occupations which were sex-segregated and popularly defined as "women's work." Nearly three out of four female professionals entered either elementary school teaching or nursing. Women in factories were most likely to be found running looms in textile mills, making garments, or canning foodstuffs. By 1930 typing and stenography had become almost completely "women's work," and 30 percent of the female labor force listed themselves as clerical workers. For women who worked, there was clearly a "place" in the job market as well as in the home.

One of the presumptions which went along with that "place" was that women neither needed nor deserved to be paid in the same way as men. The average female worker rarely earned more than 50 to 65 percent of what men received. Domestic workers received less than a dollar a day and women working in southern mill towns in 1929 earned only $9.35 a week. Even where men and women held the same jobs, the pay disparity was wide. In 1939 male social workers received an average salary of $1,718.00, women $1,442.00. A male finisher in the paper-box industry in New York City earned $35.50 a week, a female doing the same work only half as much. Throughout, the assumption was that women were working only for "pin money." Since woman's true "place" was in the home where a father or husband provided support, those women who worked allegedly were doing so only to secure extra cash for frivolous desires. Hence, it was possible to rationalize low wage rates on the basis that women did not really need their earnings to live on. In fact, Women's Bureau studies showed that in the 1920s and 1930s approximately 90 percent of employed females went to work because of economic need and used their income to support themselves and their families.

A corollary assumption was that under no circumstances should a woman be in a position competitive with or superior to that of a man. Women factory workers were rarely promoted to positions of supervision, and female professionals frequently were excluded from bar associations and professional clubs. Although women comprised over 80 percent of the nation's teachers by 1940, they served as superintendents of schools in only 45 out of 2,853 cities. Similarly, despite the fact that women made up 75 percent of the membership of the International Ladies Garment Workers Union, only one female served on the twenty-four person board of the union. Consistently, women seeking better treatment met harsh resistance. When women unionists accused the AFL of prejudice against females in 1921, Samuel Gompers replied that the International Unions discriminated against any "nonassimilable race."

The most pervasive manifestation of traditional attitudes was the nearly universal opposition to the employment of middle-class wives. In the eyes of most Americans, marriage itself was a woman's primary career, and anyone who tried to combine an outside profession with the occupation of mother and housewife received little support. As late as 1920 only 12.2 percent of all professional women were married, and 75 percent of the women who earned doctorates between 1877 and 1924 remained single. Since all women theoretically wished to marry, employers frequently refused to consider giving women important positions lest they become engaged and leave the job. The result was a double bind. As one executive wrote in the 1920s, the "highest profession a woman can engage in is that of a charming wife and wise mother." With that belief as a premise, there was little possibility that women of opposite intentions would receive much encouragement. Even educators defended the status quo. "One of the chief ends of a college for women is to fit them to become the makers of homes," the president of Union College told a Skidmore audience in 1925. "Whatever else a woman may be, the highest purpose of her life always has been to strengthen and beautify and sanction the home." In such a situation, the woman who wished to be different faced an almost impossible task. Carol Kennecott, the heroine of Sinclair Lewis' *Main Street*, desperately craved some career or involvement outside the home for herself, but as Lewis observed, "to the village doctor's wife, [outside employment] was taboo." Throughout the first four decades of the twentieth century, it was permissible for wives of poor people, immigrants, or blacks to work. But for the average middle-class white wife, holding a job was frowned upon as fundamentally inconsistent with her social status and a negative reflection on the ability of her husband to fulfill his role as "provider."

Although there were many reasons for the absence of change in women's status, the most profound was the extent to which behavior and attitudes reinforced each other and were embedded in the daily process of living. Middle-class boys were raised to consider themselves breadwinners, girls to think of themselves as homemakers. Success for the one meant holding a job, being strong, and earning the respect of his colleagues; success for the other meant marriage, a happy home, and motherhood. There were few models for men or women who wished to depart from the norm. Given the discrimination built into the economic structure as well as the forces of socialization, it was not surprising that most women conformed to the status quo, or that those who were forced to work were treated as a marginal and subservient group.

The Impact of World War II

In the overall history of women and work in America, World War II stands as the most decisive breaking point. The eruption of hostilities generated an unprecedented demand for new workers and new production. As had been true in the past, the urgency of defeating an enemy swept aside, temporarily at least, traditional attitudes which confined women to the home. A massive public relations campaign playing on the theme of patriotism called women of all ages into the job market only a few years after women had been told to stay in the home lest they interfere with a man's capacity to earn a living. Female employment became a national necessity instead of a social aberration.

The statistics on female participation in the labor force suggest the measure of change which took place. In four years more than six million women entered the job market, increasing the female labor force by 57 percent. In 1940, 25.6 percent of all women were employed. By the end of the war that figure had shot up to 36 percent, a larger increase in four years than had taken place in the previous four decades combined. "Rosie the Riveter" was only the most obvious example of the contribution women workers made. Whether cutting down trees, maintaining railroad tracks, filing military orders in offices, ferrying airplanes, or planting crops, women served skillfully in almost every job which existed. Understandably, the most dramatic increases in employment came in war related industries where in four years the num-

ber of women workers skyrocketed 460 percent. (There had been
26 women employed in the construction of ships in December
1939. By 1943 that figure had climbed to 126,000.) But the increases were not limited to war industries alone. Over two million women went to work in offices during the war, half of them
for Uncle Sam. By 1945 women constituted 38 percent of all federal workers, more than twice the percentage of the last prewar
year.

From a social point of view, however, the most important fact
about World War II was that the women who went to work were
married and over thirty-five. Prior to 1940 the vast majority of
employed women were young, single, and poor. The place of a
married woman, it was thought, was in the home. But as one
government official observed in 1943, "employers, like other individuals, are finding it necessary to weigh old values, old institutions, in terms of the world at war." Nowhere was this observation more accurate than in the case of married women in the
work force. Nearly three out of four of the new women workers
were married, and the number of wives in the labor force doubled between 1940 and 1945. Similarly, more than 60 percent of
those who took jobs were over thirty-five. By the end of the war
it was just as likely for a wife over forty to be employed as for a
single woman under twenty-five, and the proportion of all married women who were employed had jumped from 15.2 percent
to more than 24 percent.

At the time, of course, most observers expected that these
women would return to the home happily as soon as the crisis
had ended. Indeed, most of the workers themselves expressed
such a feeling when they first went on the job. But by the end of
the war, a remarkable thing had happened: many of the women
workers found that they enjoyed their jobs, that they welcomed
the opportunity to associate with others in the office or on the
assembly line, and that they valued the paycheck which was their
reward. In a Women's Bureau survey conducted in 1944 and
1945, between 75 and 80 percent of all war workers indicated
their strong desire to remain on the job after the fighting had
stopped. As one worker said, "war jobs have uncovered unsus-
pected abilities in American women. Why lose all these abilities
because of a belief that 'a woman's place is in the home.' For
some it is, for others not."

Although demobilization brought a substantial loss of jobs for
women workers (and men as well), many of the underlying

changes initiated during the war remained in effect and continued to develop. By 1950 there were twice as many women employed in California as there had been in 1940, and nationwide, the proportion of women at work had jumped from 25 percent to more than 30 percent. Nor did the sharp rise in female employment slow down thereafter. During the 1950s the employment of women increased at a rate four times faster than that of men and in 1960 twice as many women were on the job as in 1940. By the mid-1970s, 45 percent of all women over sixteen were in the labor force and there seemed little reason to doubt that the percentage would continue to grow.

Most important, however, was the fact that the major increases came among those who first joined the labor force in large numbers during World War II. By 1952 some 10.4 million wives held jobs—2 million more than at the height of World War II and almost three times the number employed in 1940. The proportion of married women in the labor force increased from 15 percent in 1940 to 30 percent in 1960 and again to 40 percent by 1970. While the percentage of single women who worked remained constant over thirty years (approximately 50 percent), the proportion for married women grew almost three times from 1940 to 1970.

Much of this change, in turn, came from the middle-aged group who had first found it respectable to enter employment during the war. Two and a half million women over thirty-three went to work between 1940 and 1950 and the median age of female workers rose from thirty-two to thirty-six and a half. By 1970 more than 50 percent of all women from thirty-five to fifty-four years of age held jobs—a figure comparable to that for young women between eighteen and twenty-four years old. These were the middle-aged women whom Margaret Mead described in 1953 as feeling "restless and discontented. . . unwanted and rudderless" once the task of raising a family was over. A job for them provided a new life, new friends, and a valued sense of contributing something important to the world. It was not surprising, then, that by 1970 more than half of all women with children in school (age six through seventeen) worked either part-time or full-time.

Perhaps most significant, the women who took jobs in the years after 1940 tended increasingly to come from the middle class. The war itself, of course, legitimized employment for people of all social and economic backgrounds. In addition, the

rapid growth of clerical work and white-collar occupations created positions which were not inconsistent with middle-class status. The continued growth of the white-collar sector of the economy coincided with the rapid increase in female employment
among middle-class women. Rising aspirations, infectious con-
sumerism, the desire to send John or Jill to a good college, and
the spiral of inflation all did their part to make continued employment of middle-class women a necessity for living the "good
life" in America.

The result was that for millions of American families female
employment became a crucial means by which to achieve and
maintain a middle-class standard of living. Prior to 1940 the employment of married women had been limited almost completely
to families with a poverty level income. By 1954, in contrast, the
National Manpower Council reported that in 40 percent of all
families with a total income of $6,000 to $10,000 a year, both the
husband and wife worked. By 1964 a larger proportion of wives
worked when their husbands received $7,500 to $10,000 per year
(42 percent) than when their spouses earned under $3,000 (37
percent), and by 1970, 60 percent of all nonfarm wives in families with incomes over $10,000 were employed. Participation in
the labor force also correlated directly with educational level so
that 70 percent of those women with more than four years of
higher education held jobs as opposed to only 30 percent of
those with an eighth grade education.

As a result of all these forces, the shape of the female labor
force was drastically altered. To be sure, the vast majority of
women continued to work in sex-segregated occupations, concen-
trating in service industries, clerical jobs, government positions,
manufacturing, teaching, and nursing. The major change had
been toward more white-collar jobs and fewer blue-collar jobs.
But the women who held these positions were a vastly different
group than those who had been employed in 1940. Prior to
World War II, employment for the white, married, middle-class
woman was virtually unheard of. Thirty years later, it had become the norm for many women through most of their lives.
World War II had not caused the change in direct way, but it
had created the context in which a different pattern of behavior
evolved. It provided a crucial catalyst toward breaking up an old
system of economic roles and setting in motion a new one.

The Persistence of Traditional Attitudes, 1940 through 1965

If anything was more striking than the changes in the female labor force, it was the persistence of traditional attitudes toward woman's proper "place." During the war itself, women were consistently denied the opportunity to take part in high-level policy decisions or to hold top management posts. As Mary Anderson, Director of the Women's Bureau noted, women had been put "off in a corner." A pattern of discrimination also continued in wage policy. Although the National War Labor Board issued a directive calling for equal pay for equal work, the order contained enough loopholes so that employers in most cases could continue to discriminate in their wage scales. Thus, for example, General Motors paid women less than men simply by substituting the categories "heavy" and "light" for "male" and "female."

One of the most controversial issues involving women during the war centered on the question of providing day care facilities for the children of mothers who worked. As long as society expected women to bear primary responsibility for the home and children, there was no way in which females could compete equally with males without some assistance in the form of community services. The need for day care centers during the war was obvious. Over 60 percent of the women hired by the war department, for example, had children of school or preschool age. Government observers estimated that the problem of child care or family responsibilities was the number one cause of absenteeism of women workers. In addition, newspapers were full of sensational reports of children being exiled to movie theaters or locked in parked cars in factory parking lots while their mothers went to work. On the other hand, providing public support for day care violated traditional assumptions that mothers should be in the home rather than in the work force. Millions of Americans agreed with the Children's Bureau official who declared: "A mother's primary duty is to her home and children. This duty is one she cannot lay aside, no matter what the emergency." Although the government did embark upon a day care program, it barely made a dent in the need which existed. Money was part of the problem; bureaucratic infighting also served as an obstacle; but the ultimate problem was a value conflict over whether, and how the government should encourage mothers to seek work.

Once the war was over a concerted effort developed to defend traditional values. The war had produced social instability, unprecedented migration, and the break-up of families. Many Americans wished to reestablish the fundamental ground rules of society. One sociologist, in a widely circulated magazine article, insisted that if women continued to work, children would be neglected and the home would be endangered. His solution was a restoration of the patriarchal family. "Women must bear and rear children," he argued, "husbands must support them."

Pursuing the same theme, Ferdinand Lundberg and Marynia Farnham contended in a best-selling book that what was at stake was woman's true femininity. Female employment, they contended in *Modern Woman: The Lost Sex,* was part of a feminist neurosis which caused women to reject their natural instincts toward motherhood, and substitute instead an effort to become imitation men. According to this view, women had been created to be biologically and psychologically dependent on men. Hence, the independent woman was "a contradiction in terms." The only way women could achieve true happiness, Lundberg and Farnham concluded, was to reenter the home with enthusiasm, take up anew the lost arts of canning and preserving, devote their entire energies to husbands and children, and achieve a "higher role" as modern wives and mothers.

Similar arguments dominated much of the mass media. Magazines during the 1950s celebrated the virtues of "togetherness," and advertisers attempted to sell their product by showing families with four children—the "average" American family—out on a picnic or vacation. Public opinion polls showed that the vast majority of Americans did not question the traditional allocation of sex roles and believed that a woman's primary place was in the home. A visitor from another planet who read the magazines and newspapers of the 1950s would never have guessed that the women portrayed as being engaged exclusively in homemaking activities were also joining the job market in unprecedented numbers.

Ironically, the gap between traditional attitudes and actual behavior probably facilitated the continued expansion of the female labor force. If women workers had been perceived as participants in a feminist crusade to achieve equality with men and thus to challenge traditional values, it is unlikely that they would have been allowed so easily into the work force. On the other hand, the fact that they were working to send children to college, to cope with inflation, or to get the money for a new car or house meant that their activity could be interpreted as consistent with woman's primary role as "helpmate" to the family. Significantly, the vast majority of women who worked cited "economic need" as the basis for their employment, even in situations where the family income was well into the middle-class range. The idea that women were working temporarily to help meet an immediate need served as a convenient and credible explanation for employment to those who might oppose in theory the idea of men and women as equal participants in the outside world.

In the meantime, the continued expansion of the female labor force inevitably affected the overall structure of sex roles, and indirectly at least, prepared the foundation for an attack on traditional values. Wherever married women worked, sociologists found that husbands performed more household chores, and that power within the family was shared to a greater extent between the man and woman, particularly on major economic issues. Neither of these shifts was ideologically inspired, nor was equality ever approached. But social scientists concluded unanimously that female employment was crucial in fostering a greater overlapping of sex roles. Other studies showed that the daughters of mothers who worked scored lower on traditional femininity scales than the daughters of mothers who did not work, and were more likely to see men and women as enacting a variety of work, recreational, and home roles. The evidence suggested that in those households where both parents worked, the children were likely to grow up with a different set of expectations about woman's "place," than in traditional homes. As the sociologist Robert Blood has observed,

> Employment emancipates women from domination by their husbands and secondarily raises daughters from inferiority with their brothers. . . . The classic differences between masculinity and femininity are disappearing as both sexes in the adult generation take on the same roles in the labor market.

Although Blood's comment was exaggerated, it seemed that even as traditional attitudes remained intact, the expansion of the female work force was helping to provide the foundation for challenging those values.

The Women's Liberation Movement and the Economic Status of Women

By the end of the 1960s, the revival of feminism made it impossible to ignore any longer the inequality experienced by American women. The movement for women's liberation drew from many currents, but one of the most important was the civil rights movement. The struggle for Negro rights highlighted the immorality of discriminating against anyone on the basis of physical characteristics. As women watched black Americans struggle for their freedom, they quickly perceived the relevance of the civil rights movement to their own situation. Just as important, the leaders of the younger wing of the woman's liberation movement were driven to seek their own emancipation on the basis of their experience within the movement. They had joined the demonstrations to free blacks, only to find that they were assigned subservient roles in the movement, asked to do menial chores, and denied any participation in the policy-making process. When the women of the Student Non-Violent Coordinating Committee (SNCC) gathered together to protest, they inaugurated a pattern of response which was soon to spread throughout the student movement and gradually across the country as small groups of women met to share their common grievances and concerns in "consciousness-raising"sessions.

A second current of the movement grew out of the increasing alienation of middle-class business and professional women. Angered by continued discrimination and inspired by the model of civil rights protest as well, these women joined in organizations like the National Organization of Women (NOW) to push for concrete legislative and economic action which would bring closer the goal of equality. The discontent of both female students and older women had been spurred by the publication in 1963 of Betty Friedan's *The Feminine Mystique*. Writing with passion and eloquence, Friedan protested against the fact that women's entire life was circumscribed by the condition of their birth. Men had multiple opportunities to prove themselves in a variety of occupations, Friedan argued, but women were consigned involuntarily to the biologicaly defined roles of wife and mother. Friedan's vivid descriptions of "the problem that has no name" gave to millions of women a new recognition that what concerned them was not just a personal problem but a social issue.

As the various segments of the woman's movement mounted their protests, they built upon the change which had already taken place. As John Kenneth Galbraith pointed out in *The Affluent Society*, conventional ideas become most vulnerable when the "march of events" makes them outdated and irrelevant. Ever since World War II the *reality* of woman's "place" had ceased to conform to the *stereotype*. As the gap between theory and fact grew ever wider, a social foundation was created for the attack on old ideas and the development of new ones. Feminists over the decades had been saying much the same thing as Betty Friedan, but in the 1960s an audience was ready to respond to the message. Although the economic role of women had changed, inequality remained as omnipresent as ever. Now, a movement set out to attack the ideas responsible for perpetuating that inequality.

The genius of the women's movement was its multiplicity. Avoiding the Achilles' heel of earlier women's movements, it did not tie itself to a single issue nor seek change in just one segment of life. Instead, it operated in a decentralized fashion in local communities where women could devote their energies to whatever issue involved them most. The spectrum of concerns was almost endless, from writing children's books which eliminated invidious sexual stereotypes to starting day care centers or running free health clinics. Significantly, though, almost every program of the movement bore some relationship to the issue of women's position in the economy. Using Title VII of the 1964 Civil Rights Act which prohibited economic discrimination on the basis of sex, national organizations like NOW worked effectively to tear down ancient barriers which excluded women from equal access to good jobs. The federal government was pressured into investigating widespread discrimination in colleges and universities against women, and then into devising programs to end it. Through court suits or the threat of them, huge corporations were persuaded to institute programs of affirmative action involving the hiring of women. On a local level, groups which worked for better day care acted in an area decisive to the question of whether women would have the opportunity to pursue careers or take jobs while their children were still of a preschool age. The right to choose, or not choose, an abortion similarly affected in a direct way women's chance of determining their own career plans, and the writing of new children's books had as an ultimate goal giving girls and boys a variety of work and family models to follow.

Perhaps most important, the widespread discussion about the issues of women's liberation made a whole generation profoundly aware of the possibilities which should be open to those women who wished to pursue life plans different from previous patterns. Once raised to a level of conscious reflection and awareness, the issue of women's rights could not easily be set aside. Public opinion surveys provided the most dramatic confirmation of the change. As late as 1962, only a minority of women in a Gallup Poll believed that women were treated unfairly. Eight years later, women respondents were still divided equally on the question. By 1974, in contrast, women approved by a margin of two to one the effort to improve their status and secure equality. The level of support was even higher among younger women. Even where women expressed some reservation about the movement *per se* as "too radical," they generally gave strong endorsement to feminist programs such as day care centers, equal pay, and the right to abortion.

By the mid-1970s, a whole constellation of social and economic forces had come together to insure a continuing transformation in the status of women. Although it was difficult to single out one variable as decisive, each element in the overall picture reinforced the others, creating a total pattern which indicated significant departures in both the family and the work force.

First, the birthrate had reached a level of zero population growth. After World War II, the birthrate had skyrocketed as young couples began to have families which had been deferred during the war. The "baby boom" continued to the early fifties, reaching a peak in 1957. There then ensued a prolonged downturn which in 1967 resulted in a birthrate of 17.9 per thousand persons compared to more than 25 per thousand a decade earlier. Although experts predicted that the "baby boom" of the fifties would have an echo effect in the late sixties and seventies when the children born twenty years earlier began to reproduce, the opposite happened. Instead of rising, the birthrate reached an all-time low in 1972, 1973, and 1974. The change could best be seen in two Gallup Polls, one in 1967, the other in 1971. The earlier survey showed that 34 percent of women in the prime childbearing years anticipated having four or more children. By

1971, in contrast, the figure had dropped to 15 percent. All indicators pointed to a continued low birthrate.

Second, this decline coincided with a trend toward later marriages. By 1971 more than half of all women twenty years of age were single in contrast to only one-third in 1960, and the number of unmarried women in the twenty to twenty-four age bracket had climbed from 28 percent in 1960 to 37 percent a decade later. In the 60s the proportion of women between twenty and thirty-four living alone or with roommates increased by 109 percent.

Simultaneously, the greatest increase in the female labor force during the 1960s and 1970s took place among younger women of childbearing age. The proportion of women working in the twenty to twenty-four year old age group increased from 50 percent in 1964 to 61 percent in 1973. The percentage for the twenty-five to thirty-five year old group rose from 37 to 50 percent, including 75 percent of those women without children. In the twenty to twenty-four year old group, 86 percent of women college graduates were employed as opposed to 71 percent fourteen years earlier. But the fastest rise of all took place among women with young children. From 1959 through 1974, the employment rate for mothers with children under three more than doubled, from 15 to 31 percent, and that for mothers of children three to five years old increased from 25 to 39 percent. By the mid-1970s, the labor force participation rate of women in the prime childbearing years had caught up with the employment percentages of women in almost every other age group and had surpassed the participation rate of the most active age groups twenty years earlier. In fact, there appears to have been a simple cultural logic at work in the employment patterns of women since World War II. Those who first broke the barriers against married women's employment were middle aged. With no children in the home, they posed the least threat to traditional ideas of women's "place" as homemakers and mothers. Later, a major increase in employment occurred among mothers with children six to seventeen years of age. By the late sixties, in turn, the major change took place among mothers of younger children. It was almost as though each step in the process was necessary to prepare the way for the next one, until by the mid-1970s there was a consistent departure from the traditional norm of mothers staying at home full-time to care for children.

Finally, at the end of the 1960s, women college students demonstrated a rapidly rising interest in careers, including those not traditionally viewed as "women's work." Between 1969 and 1973, the proportion of women students in law schools increased from 6 percent to 16 percent, and many experts believed that the figure would grow to nearly 50 percent by the 1980s. Applications to medical school and schools of architecture similarly mounted. There seemed to be a new commitment on the part of women college students to carve out their own careers and, while not renouncing marriage, to view family life as only one part of their multiple interests. Between 1968 and 1980 the number of women college graduates was expected to increase by two-thirds (twice the rate of increase for men), providing a growing pool of potential career women.

Each of these forces contributed to a "multiplier effect" where shifting values interacted with changing economic conditions to create a new pattern of family and work life. During the late sixties, women married later, delayed the birth of their first child, and bore their last child at an earlier age. Whether as cause or effect, this trend coincided with many women finding careers and interests outside of the home. The rewards of having a job and extra money tended to emphasize the advantages of a small family and the freedom to travel, entertain, or pursue individual career interests. Surrounding all these developments, in turn, was the cultural impact of the woman's movement and its challenge to traditional values. For the first time in many decades, it appeared that behavior and attitudes were moving in the same direction. Not surprisingly, the shape of women's participation in the labor force came close to matching that of men by the mid-1970s, and in some age groups, women's participation in the labor force had already exceeded the Department of Labor's projections for the year 1990. On the basis of historical trends, there seemed little doubt that continued change in women's economic status would dominate the history of the last decades of the twentieth century, exerting a profound impact on the family, the economy, social values, and women's definition of themselves.

The Issue of Equality

Even given the changes which had taken place, it was foolish to underestimate the obstacles to equality or overestimate the progress which had been made. The average earnings of women had actually declined relative to men rather than risen. Although some barriers to equal opportunity in higher education had been eliminated through HEW enforcement proceedings, most patterns of discrimination remained intact. Above all, cultural presumptions about woman's "place" continued to pervade the society. When people are raised with a set of attitudes and ideas as deeply embedded as those about sex roles, inequities rarely disappear quickly.

The basic issue, of course, was how equality was defined. For more than two hundred years the word had been associated almost indistinguishably with liberty and freedom as part of the American creed. Most Americans saw no contradiction between the concepts, believing that they were encompassed by the overall idea of "equality of opportunity." Thus, Thomas Jefferson wrote, America would develop a natural aristocracy based upon each individual having the same opportunity to maximize his talents. The concept of equality applied to people enjoying common rights, and the concept of freedom involved the individual's use of those rights to achieve a particular goal.

Historically, therefore, the idea of equality in America has involved procedural rights rather than the substantive condition of sharing wealth, power, and resources. Throughout the nineteenth and twentieth centuries, reform groups worked to gain access to the opportunity structure for those who had been economically or politically disenfranchised. Thus, civil rights groups sought guarantee of the right to vote, access to public accommodations, and an end to economic discrimination. Women protestors focused in a similar way on the franchise and legal protection. Once overt discrimination was ended, it was thought, the individual bore primary responsibility for using the rights shared in common with others to advance his or her own cause.

By the end of the 1960s, however, the concept of equal opportunity as an adequate goal had come under increasing attack. Critics argued that only if everyone started in fact from the same social and economic place could the idea of equal opportunity retain credibility. But as Lyndon Johnson pointed out, it made little sense to talk about equality of opportunity to black people when as a group they stood in the valley looking up, while white people as a group stood on a plateau looking down. Women as well as blacks and other minority groups began to concentrate their energies on securing more of the substance of equality, or at least a more solid base from which to seek individual goals. In

the case of women, this involved the demand for publicly supported day care centers so that women might have access to the
job market, and the institution of affirmative action programs to
guarantee women consideration as potential candidates for job
openings. In short, there developed a new realization that equality was an empty word without collective action to insure greater
sharing of wealth, power, and resources.

The question of equality was further complicated by the long
range economic situation facing the world. After the longest period of prosperity in the country's history, it seemed by the mid-
1970s that unlimited growth had come to an end. The energy
crisis represented the most visible symptom of the new reality. In
an economy where one of every seven jobs was related to the automobile industry, it seemed clear that a shortage of fuel would
automatically mean a curtailment of the growth rate which had
obtained in the country since World War II. Ever since the nation had begun, Americans had conceived of their wealth as an
infinite pie. Since there was no end to the possibility of growth,
there was no reason why the advance of one group should take
place at the expense of another. By the time of the bicentennial,
however, there was a new sense that the pie was finite and that
some hard decisions would have to be made about how to dis-
tribute the pieces.

In this context, the demand of women for equality posed significant ideological as well as practical questions for American
society. American institutions celebrated individualism, competition, free enterprise, and winning. American males, in particular,
grew up with the belief that coming in first was what counted,
that one should always strive to beat out the nearest competitor,
and that in the job market especially, it was strength and achievement which counted. Now, a growing segment of the population
was arguing that the collective good was more important than
individual accomplishment, that cooperation should take the
place of competition, and that a more equitable distribution of
power and resources was necessary if a majority of the population was to have the opportunity for personal fulfillment.

On a public or institutional level, the conflict of values centered on how quickly and effectively government, business,
schools, and labor would implement programs to make real the
theoretical commitment to equal rights of men and women. How,
for example, would labor and management handle the question
of seniority, particularly in a time of recession when the last hi-

red—women or blacks—would ordinarily be the first fired? Would universities and corporations give *pro forma* acquiescence to affirmative action, or would they make a genuine effort to search out female and black candidates for job positions? What would be the response of the courts to the growing probability of a direct clash between the rights of individuals and the demands of groups for more equitable treatment? Would government and business boost the possibilities of achieving equality by instituting more flexible job hours so that men and women, on a part-time basis, could find the room to meet both their job and home responsibilities? Would the government and voluntary associations create quality day care centers for young children and guard against a proliferation of poor custodial care? And how would political leaders, the mass media, and the educational establishment respond when such measures came under attack for being a subversion of "the American way" and the doctrines of free enterprise and individualism?

On a personal and family level, the issues became, if anything, even more complicated. Would men and women in a relationship be able to take turns making sacrifices so that the other had a possibility of pursuing her or his individual goals? Would a husband who was a junior executive and rising rapidly in a corporation be willing to take a year's leave of absence so that his wife could resume her studies at law school? Conversely, would a woman who was just embarked on a medical career be able and willing to go on a part-time schedule so that her husband could earn a doctorate? How would children be raised so that they would have both the sense of being loved by their parents and a feeling of pride in the accomplishments of their mother and father? What would be the response of men brought up to believe in the "masculine mystique," when they were asked to embrace a different set of values? Where would the communities of support come from to give men and women the courage to embark upon new forms of career and family interaction? Above all, would there develop enough ideological commitment to a new set of values to sustain men and women and their relationships through the tension and stress which would inevitably accompany change?

Needless to say, these and other questions had no easy answers. The terrain was new, and there were few guideposts to show the way. But for the first time in the nation's history the question of equality between the sexes ranked high on the agenda of social issues. How the question was answered depended ultimately both on external social institutions and interior, personal value choices. Whatever the final result, few decisions promised to have greater significance for the future of the society.

Karl E. Taeuber and James A. Sweet

2

Family and Work:

The Social Life Cycle of Women

The Life-Cycle Approach

"All the world's a stage and all the men and women merely players. They have their exits and their entrances, and one man in his time plays many parts." Thus did Shakespeare begin his description of the changing roles a person plays as time and age march on. A life-cycle perspective also guides our discussion of women's roles in the contemporary United States. Our medium, alas, is neither poetry nor drama, but descriptive demography. We shall identify a few major stages and processes in the life cycle—completion of schooling, leaving the parental home, entry into the world of paid work, marriage and formation of one's own family, and the eventual dissolution of that family. We shall indicate the typical timing of these events in the life cycle and something of the way in which each stage or process may overlap and interfere with another.

Our special interest in this chapter is the process of participation by women in the labor force, by which we mean working or seeking to work for pay. Participation in the labor force is not as bound to a particular age span in the life cycle as are completion

KARL E. TAEUBER. *Professor of Sociology at the University of Wisconsin, is co-author of* Negroes in Cities *and* Migration in the United States. JAMES A. SWEET. *Professor of Sociology at the University of Wisconsin, is author of* Women in the Labor Force *and has written articles on marriage, marital disruption, and fertility.*

of schooling, marriage, childbearing, childrearing, presiding over
the empty nest, and widowhood. Labor force participation may
coincide with each of these life-cycle stages, or none, or any com-
bination.

Shakespeare portrayed the life cycle of prototypical man. In
our mundane portrayal of modern American woman we speak
not of essences that remain eternal but of specific events and se-
quences that are subject to change. What was typical a generation ago may no longer be so. The working woman, a statistical
minority in the first half of the twentieth century, became a statistical majority during the third quarter of the century. This is the
transformation that will occupy our center stage. We shall be particularly interested in evidence on changes in the timing and incidence of labor force participation and of other social events in
the life cycle.

Change, we are repeatedly told, is endemic in the modern
world. It is not confined to a single one of life's activities, such as
work, but occurs in many. The very pattern of relationships
among activities is itself subject, indeed compelled, to change.
For example, from late in the nineteenth century until the middle
of the twentieth, there was a gradual decline in the typical age at
first marriage among American women. There was also a steady
rise in the average level of education. As the typical age at marriage moved downward and the typical age at leaving school
moved upward, more and more women faced in their own lives a
potential or actual conflict between staying in school and getting
married. Whatever the degree of conflict and whatever alternatives chosen for its resolution, millions of women were undoubtedly compelled to think about education and marriage in a new,
deliberate, and self-conscious way.

Recent rapid changes in female labor force participation rate,
fertility rate, divorce rate, and other less easily quantified aspects
of women's roles and statuses have been accompanied by a complex of normative, political, and psychological change. Women's
Liberation is the expression and encouragement of this complex
collective movement. Some of the recent status changes (rising
educational attainment, for example) are continuations of very
long term trends. Other recent changes, such as declining fertility, are contemporaneous with the formative years of Women's
Lib in the 1960s, before it had become a mass movement and
before its concerns were publicized in the mass media. Still other

changes (a decline in the marriage rate) are very recent shifts in trend.

Tracing the historical pattern of short and long-term trends is a necessary prelude to assessing their significance. The perspective of twenty-five, fifty, or a hundred years of statistical history will show that many changes in women's status are co-extensive with fundamental processes of long-term demographic, social, and economic change. Some of these trends were doubtless affected by the public debate, litigation, and legislation stirred by women's liberationists of the late nineteenth and early twentieth centuries. But it is also the case that these trends themselves, with their complex causes, independent dynamic, and internal inertia, may in turn have stimulated the recent resurgence of women's rights as a major public issue. The basic data that we shall present cannot resolve the chicken and egg problem of what is cause and what is effect. With a touch of social science and demographic history we seek only to raise such questions, not to lay them to rest.

SNAPSHOTS, CROSS-SECTIONS, AND COHORTS

Most statistical data on the status of women, whether the data appear in scholarly journals, government reports, or more popular presentations, are of a snapshot variety. They are drawn from the 1970 or earlier census, or from a single national survey. Although the rates at which young women worked in 1970 may be compared to the rates at which older women worked in 1970, the perspective from such a cross-section is flawed. The older women on whom the 1970 census reports did not, when they were young, have the same characteristics that young women had in 1970. To compare young and old from a snapshot survey does not indicate the changes that occur as the young grow older.

Demographers handle the problem of making life-cycle pictures from snapshots by creating cohort data from a series of snapshots. The technique is analogous to making a movie out of a set of successive stills. A cohort is simply a set of people who were born in the same period, for example, women born in the years 1900-1909. From the 1910 census one can obtain data on the characteristics of these women as children. From the 1920 census one learns about their teenage years. From the 1930 census one learns how many were married, how many children they had in the early years of childbearing, and whether those with and without children were gainfully employed. Further stages in the life cycle of this cohort are described in the 1940 census data for women aged thirty to forty, in the 1950 census data for women aged forty to fifty, in the 1960 census data for women aged fifty to sixty, and in the 1970 census data for women aged sixty to seventy. A similar technique can be used with annual survey data to trace out trends for narrower portions of the life cycle over shorter time periods. To the extent that the available data permit such rearrangement into cohort form, we are able to maintain a life-cycle perspective on recent history.

Our review of recent trends begins with the fundamental demographic life cycle—birth and death—and moves quickly to what has become known as the family life cycle. In this section attention focuses on the age of occurrence of the basic events of family formation (marriage), family expansion (childbirth), and family dissolution (children leaving home and spouse dying). Succeeding sections will add other dimensions—leaving home, completing an education, and holding a job. Each of these will be considered separately. But as discussion of the broader social life cycle proceeds the analysis will become more complex. In the modern world getting married or having children has little effect on the age at which one dies, but there is no such independence for most of the events of the social life cycle. Marriage and childbearing are linked, however imperfectly, and one's residence, education, marital status, number and age of children, and participation in the labor force are all interconnected. We shall portray some of these connections, but in a final section we will indicate how incomplete our discussion has been, how much more complex and interesting the real world is than are our tabulations of average ages and average women, and how other attributes and events omitted from our account further enrich the human experience.

The Demographic and Family Life Cycles

THE MORTALITY REVOLUTION

At the time of the nation's centennial, the average age at death for women was less than fifty years. At the time of the bicentennial, the female life span has been extended to nearly eighty years. In the modern experience it is normal for death to occur in old age, after a woman has long since completed her reproductive cycle, her childraising activities, and her productive employment. Death terminates the life cycle after all the other stages of great social and economic interest have been passed by. It is typically an ending, often a welcome one, to a full and complete life.

The transition to a low-mortality society affected the family life cycle deeply. When the average age at death was less than fifty years, death typically took at least one parent before the children were all grown. Giving birth was itself a life-threatening activity for women. Death rates in the childbearing years have been cut by 90 percent, and deaths directly resulting from childbearing have become rare events. One hundred years ago one of every five newborn died in infancy, and families considered themselves lucky if all their children survived to adulthood. Today the survival of an infant is almost taken for granted.

The conquest of early death is not simply ancient history. It is a process that occurred in the United States during the lifetime of persons who are still alive. The fall of mortality is responsible for steady increases in the numbers and proportions of women who survive to have the opportunity to consider paid employment after the children are all of school age or after they are grown. The fall of mortality is responsible for the enormous increase in numbers and proportions of old couples and widows dependent on pensions and social security. The fall of mortality in all likelihood fostered an increasing sense of control over one's fate that in turn is a factor in the secularization of marriage, the practice of techniques to control the number and timing of births, and the willingness to invest for the future. The demographic transition that is producing population explosion and social change around the world is still a recent event in our national history. The social consequences of fundamental demographic change take generations to be fully worked out.

In Figure 1 the age of occurrence of typical life-cycle events is shown for seven successive ten-year cohorts of women, born from 1880-1889 to 1940-1949. The mortality revolution appears in this chart primarily in the increasing gap between the top two lines—first marriage of last child and death of one spouse. The lines on this figure are true cohort estimates, not simply snapshots. Women born in the 1880s reached age fifty-six to fifty-seven, the average age of death of spouse or self and of first marriage of last child, around the year 1940, so this portion of the figure is based on mortality levels prevailing in 1940. The sharply higher mortality levels of 1910 and 1880 affected the final portion of the family life cycle for earlier cohorts of women, whose experience is not represented in the figure. Only the recent impact of the mortality revolution is revealed here. But the high-mortality society in which lived our grandmothers, and even more the grandmothers of our grandmothers, passed on to us a set of traditional values and attitudes that do not grant women a formal role outside the home and family.

Fig. 1. Stages of the Family Life Cycle

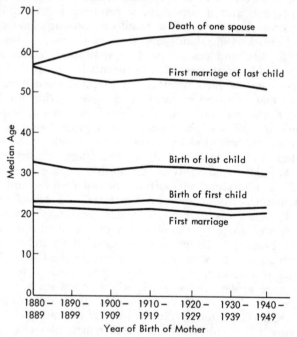

FAMILY FORMATION AND EXPANSION

The lower lines in Figure 1 indicate the median age at which successive cohorts of women experienced the early stages of family formation and expansion. There is a striking consistency throughout our recent history in the timing of these events in the life cycle. This consistency in timing conceals, as we shall see in later sections, marked changes in the proportion of women who marry, the proportion who remain childless in marriage, and the number of children born to the average family. The first cohort included in the figure does have a higher age at birth of last child, a result of the generally higher fertility early in this century.

The cohort of women born in 1910-1919 displays a slight rise in the age of marriage and childbearing. These women reached adulthood during the great depression. Their completed family size was the smallest of any of the cohorts shown. The cohort born in 1950-1959 seems likely to set a new low, but their childbearing years are still in process and experts differ on what their fertility will be as they move through the last of their reproductive years. Hence we have not plotted estimates of the timing of this cohort's family life cycle.

The baby boom of the late 1940s and 1950s is apparent in Figure 1 only with close reading. The cohorts born in the 1920s and 1930s, themselves the reproductive outcome of a period of very low birth rates, entered marriage and childbearing quickly and in record proportions. There is a slight dip in age at first marriage and only a short interval before birth of first child. The length of time between first and last child increased, but because these women shortened the time interval between successive children their aggregate childbearing years increased much less sharply than did the aggregate numbers of children born to them.

FOOTLOOSE AND FANCY FREE

In a society organized as a network of nuclear families, children grow up in one family and upon reaching adulthood leave to form a new family. In the model of the family life cycle pictured in Figure 1, there is an implicit assumption that the transfer from one family to another is made without interlude, without a period of independent nonfamilial living. The figure seems based on an assumption that a girl remains in her parental family until she is married, that she thereupon establishes a new home, and that her own days of active childcare begin very quickly and continue until the oldest child is finally married. Such an assumption is compatible with a traditional view of the female life cycle. A similar figure for males, by contrast, would be out of keeping with the presumed period of striking out on one's own and establishing a place in the world before marriage. In fact, of course, both patterns occur for both men and women.

The timing of the between-families interlude is not shown on Figure 1 because the necessary information is lacking. To some extent this reflects a lack of data, but to a large extent it reflects the failure of scholars—even those writing entire monographs on marriage and the family—to ask the question. In the current social climate this gap in the research literature is surprising. There is a widespread presumption that the period of independence when a young woman is not tied to family plays a vital social and psychological role in developing consciousness of one's own potentialities and of alternative life paths and styles that she may choose.

A partial indication of this transitional period may be gleaned from a tally from the 1960 census showing the percentage of females who were living apart from relatives: at ages under fifteen, less than 1 percent; at ages fifteen to nineteen, 8 percent; at ages twenty to twenty-four, 11 percent; at ages twenty-five to twenty-nine, 5 percent. (For males in the same four age groups, the percentages were 1, 12, 23, and 11 respectively.) The percentages remain low during the middle adult years, and then rise sharply in old age, so that more than one-third of women who survived past age seventy-five were living apart from relatives. Few at this stage in the life cycle had any hope of forming a new family.

The tally of women living apart from relatives does not suffice to indentify the prevalence of a between-families interlude. The tally of those living with relatives includes married women living with their husbands and single women living with sisters. From special tabulations of the 1970 census we have prepared Figure 2, showing the trend for never married women to live apart from their parents. Up to age eighteen, the normal age of high school graduation, most single girls lived with their parents. Of those who were not with parents, most were with another relative or guardian or living in a college dorm, apart from but still heavily dependent on their parents. The line in Figure 2 moves steadily up. Departure of the unmarried from the parental home is a one-way process; once moved out, few move back. By their mid-twenties, about half of those who were still single had moved out of the parental nest.

Figure 2 still does not provide a full picture of the period of independence. The base population of never married females is, from a cohort perspective, steadily being depleted. Of those who remain single, increasing proportions live apart from family, but

Fig. 2. Never Married Women Living Apart from Parents , 1970

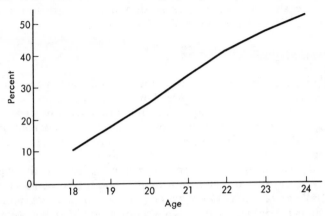

rising proportions of the total members of the cohort are, during the ages from eighteen to twenty-four, marrying and living in a new family. Combining the data portrayed in Figure 2 and a touch of speculation permits us to make some general observations.

Over a span of many decades, the shift from rural residence and agricultural employment to metropolitan residence and industrial and service employment augmented both residential and employment opportunities for young women. The shift to compulsory school attendance and nearly universal high school completion tended to keep women under age eighteen at their parental home. In recent decades the rapid increase in female postsecondary education has facilitated movement away from home. Shifts in age at first marriage, while limited in recent decades to magnitudes of only about one year in either direction, probably reduced the incidence and duration of a period of separate residence for women in the cohorts of 1920-1929 and 1930-1939 and increased it for the more recent cohorts. The net effect of all these changes was probably a higher prevalence of between-family living for women in the most recent cohorts. Yet there has been no sharp change in the overwhelming tendency for women in the young adult ages to live either with parents or with a spouse. To the extent that a new spirit of independence has developed, it must be sought not solely among the footloose living apart from families, but also among those living in filial or connubial status. If paid employment is an indicator of independence, we shall see in a later section that the greatest recent change has occurred for women in families.

Finishing School

The increasing levels of educational attainment have pushed the age at leaving school upward into the age range at which women enter first marriages. In this brief section we review trends in schooling, and in the next section we consider marriage trends and the conflict between staying in school and getting married.

At the beginning of this century, schooling beyond the eighth grade was unusual for men or women. About one of every four girls took some high school work and one of seven graduated from high school. By 1930 high school graduation had become the most common educational attainment, and it has remained so since. Schooling for successive cohorts of women is portrayed in Figure 3. (To provide more detail on recent trends, we use five-year rather than ten-year birth cohorts.) For each cohort, about half of the women graduated from high school and completed no further formal education. A substantial shift has occurred in the schooling of the other half. Members of the 1920-1924 cohort reached high school age during the depression. Dropping out of school before obtaining the high school diploma was far more common than continuing in college after high school. Among the postwar cohorts who reached high school age in the 1960s, fewer than one of five dropped out without a diploma, and more than one of every three began college.

This advance in educational levels necessarily entailed keeping more girls in school during their late teens and early twenties. To show this change more directly, the percentages of women of each age who were enrolled in school are graphed in Figure 4 for several census years. In 1970 nearly all girls under age eighteen were in school, whereas as recently as 1940 many girls at ages sixteen and seventeen were finished with school. In 1970 about half of the eighteen- and nineteen-year-old women were enrolled in school. At ages twenty to twenty-four school enrollment involved only a minority of each cohort, but the size of that minority had been increasing rapidly for several decades.

Inclusion of schooling as a life-cycle process complicates what

Fig. 3. Educational Attainment of Birth Cohorts of White Women

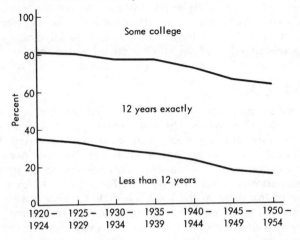

Fig. 4. School Enrollment by Age

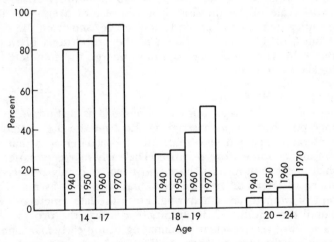

began as a straightforward review of a series of clearly separate
and sequential steps. Schooling is intended to change a person in
various ways and to alter the way she conducts her life. Educational attainment is a basic differentiating characteristic in society.
College graduates, high school graduates, and the less educated

differ in marriage rates, fertility rates, employment rates, levels of jobs, earnings, and nearly every other major social and economic characteristic. Prolongation of schooling shifts the distribution of the population along a basic dimension of social class. Thus do rising levels of educational attainment influence the life cycle in many ways not subject to documentation with demographic data.

Getting Married

Most first marriages occur within a very narrow age range in the life cycle. Throughout the last century few American women married before age eighteen, and most were married by age twenty-three. The average age at marriage, plotted in Figure 1, has shown only small fluctuations. This perception of stability in marriage patterns is belied if we shift focus from the general positioning of marriage in the total life cycle to a narrower view of the frequency and timing of marriage among successive cohorts of women as they move year by year through the late teens and early twenties. Viewed closely, there has been continuous change in nuptiality rates. The stability perceived in Figure 1 arises from the small scale of the drawing, from the use of average at marriage rather than spread around the average, and from the deliberate omission from consideration of the proportions of women who never married and hence did not undergo the complete family life cycle described.

SHIFTS IN AGE AT MARRIAGE

The cohort of women born in 1865-1874 is distinctive in the demographic history of marriage in the United States. Members of that cohort married less frequently and at later ages than was true of any cohort before or since. The early marriage pattern of colonial and pre-industrial times had been gradually replaced by a pattern of later and less frequent marriage, with as many as 9 percent of women never marrying. From the late nineteenth century until the middle of the twentieth century, the process went into a seventy year reversal, culminating in the early-marriage experience of the cohort born 1935-1939 (marrying in the late 1950s and early 1960s). The magnitude of this reversal is portrayed in Figure 5. In the years around 1970 there was another reversal, much more rapid, in which cohorts of women born after World War II and entering the prime marriage ages in the late 1960s and early 1970s delayed marriage beyond the teenage years.

Fig. 5.   *Age Pattern of Marriage for Birth Cohorts of White Women*

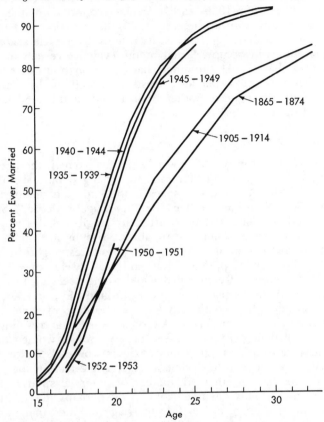

To put the recent shift in age-pattern of marriage in numerical terms, consider the percentages ever married at selected ages and compare women interviewed in the 1960 census with those interviewed in a 1974 national sample:

TABLE 1.

Age	1960	1974
18	24%	18%
20	54	42
22	74	62
24	84	77

This snapshot comparison is roughly equivalent to a comparison between the 1935-1939 early-marriage cohort and the late-marriage cohort born in the early 1950s. There is no evidence in these data that marriage has lost its role as a life-cycle stage that most women will occupy. So far as the evidence reveals to date, the recent change, like the other changes throughout the century for which data are available, consists of a shift of the marriage curve along the age-axis rather than a shift in the fundamental shape of the curve.

THE "MARRIAGE SQUEEZE"

Compared to the recent upward shift for women, the age distribution at first marriage for men has changed only slightly. A differential shift for the two sexes is the expected demographic solution to a problem called the "marriage squeeze." Single males tend to court and be courted by single females who are two or three years younger. An abrupt rise in the number of births in the nation in a given year produces, eighteen years later, a shortage of potential husbands age twenty-one for the expanded number of eighteen-year-old women seeking to marry. As women in the larger cohort move through the prime ages for first marriage, they continually face a shortage of men a few years older than themselves. An obvious societal response to such an imbalance is for increased proportions of women to delay marriage to a later age. Demographers would also expect the marriage age for men to decline as each single man in the prime marital ages has an enlarged number of potential spouses a few years younger. This did not happen, but perhaps the slight upward shift in average age at first marriage for men that was observed in the years around 1970 would have been greater in the absence of the pressures of the "marriage squeeze."

In the late 1960s and early 1970s the force of the "marriage squeeze" produced by the baby boom of the late 1940s reached its peak. As a consequence of the leveling off and subsequent decline in birth rates in the late 1950s, 1960s, and early 1970s, the demographic disequilibrium in the numbers of prospective husbands and prospective wives will diminish and then reverse direction in the late 1980s. As persons born during a period of declining birth rates reach marrying age, the supply of single men of a given age will be large relative to the smaller number of women a few years younger. Many demographers expect the coming years to bring a renewed downward adjustment in the age at marriage for women. The impact of the demographic imbalance is subject to enhancement or retardation by the operation of other social forces. A strictly demographic forecast should not be the sole ingredient stirred into one's crystal ball.

SCHOOLING VS. MARRIAGE

As a woman moves through the years from, say, age seventeen to age twenty-seven, the proportion of her cohort members who are married rapidly increases. And of those who remain single at any given age, a substantial proportion marries in the next year or two.

The precise timing of this wave of marriage varies from one cohort to another, as we have seen. It varies equally as much among women of differing educational levels within a cohort as it does among women of different cohorts. If an age-at-marriage curve is plotted for each educational level, similar to the curves in Figure 5, the curve for women who drop out of high school is farther to the left (a scale distance of about two years) than any of the curves in Figure 5. These women marry in greater numbers at younger ages than do those who obtain more education. Women who complete high school but do not continue their schooling are in the modal educational category. Their marriage curve is similar to that for the total cohort shown in Figure 5. For those women who go on to college, the marriage curve is about two years to the right.

The reasons for a strong association between education and age at marriage are so numerous and obvious that it is easy to over-explain the finding. First, many women postpone marriage until they complete whatever level of schooling they have set as their own goal. If we had sufficiently detailed data, we might find that the likelihood of marriage within, say, two years after quitting school, was very high and did not vary much according to whether a woman quit school after tenth grade, twelfth grade, sophomore year, or college graduation. A second reason is the reverse causation: a woman who gets married is likely to quit school, especially if she is or soon becomes pregnant. A third reason is the congeries of effects of education on attitudes, values, and life style, leading the more highly educated to postpone marriage. A fourth reason is the effect of family background, prior values, and personality on the education one obtains and simultaneously on the age at which one seeks to marry.

Because each successive cohort of women is staying in school longer and completing more grades of school, one would expect the age-at-marriage curve to shift to the right for the younger cohorts. The rightward shift shown in Figure 5 from the cohort of 1935-1939 to that for the cohorts of 1940-1944 and 1945-1949 can indeed be accounted for largely by the increased schooling of the more recent cohorts. Thus we can reinterpret the rightward shift for these cohorts as being primarily a consequence of trends in education, and not as indicating any large change in the age-patterning of marriage among those of a given educational level. Until more data become available on the cohorts of women born during the 1950s, we shall not know whether the continued rightward shift evident in their early years of exposure to marriage will persist as they move upward through the life cycle. The early indications (from Figure 5) suggest a larger shift than for the earlier cohorts, despite the lack of any sudden acceleration in the trend of higher educational attainment. If the trend in education accounts for most but not all of the shift among the three earlier cohorts, it will not suffice to account for the full magnitude of the latest shift.

If we attribute the recent rightward shifts of the age-at-marriage curves primarily to changing educational levels (with perhaps some other factor also important in the 1970s), how do we account for the continuing leftward shift of the curve from the cohort of 1865-1874 to that of 1935-1939? Educational improvements during that long period were substantial. Was the impact of education on age at marriage different before 1955 than after? Or was there some other reason or set of reasons that more than countered the force of education up until 1955 but that rapidly waned in impact thereafter? It is because scholars have yet to answer these questions that we referred above to the ease of "over-explaining" the association between education and age at marriage.

Although in the past many high schools prohibited married or pregnant women from attendance, such formal barriers to overlapping marriage and schooling have been falling. The barriers at the collegiate level were never so formal. Thus reasons number one and two cited above are not quite so obvious as they at first seem; such inhibiting relationships between schooling and marriage are themselves in need of explanation and trend analysis.

And the relationship itself is more complex than the simple statement "married women don't attend school." In October 1973, 6 percent of women age eighteen to twenty-one who were married and living with spouse were enrolled in school, as compared to 39 percent of women not married or in another marital category. At ages twenty-two to twenty-four, the percentage was still about 6 percent for married women living with spouse as compared to 17 percent for other women.

Here again the snapshot data on which we must so often depend fail to tell the full story. Life cycle data from a national sample of women in 1970 revealed that about one-fifth of married women under age forty-five had attended high school or college since marriage and another one-fifth expressed an intention of going back to school sooner or later. The trend toward postnuptial education seemed to be gaining strength among the younger cohorts. If we are to believe those who call on institutions of higher education to become more involved in adult and continuing education, postnuptial education may be on its way to becoming the norm rather than the exception.

Bearing and Rearing Children

Most mothers bear their successive children at relatively short intervals, one to four years apart. Thus the typical mother will have preschoolers to care for from the birth of the first child until the last-born child enters school at age five or six. On the graph of the stages of the family life cycle, Figure 1, the average age of mother at birth of first and last children is plotted. The interval of responsibility for preschool children can be determined by plotting another line about six years above the line for birth of last child. This line would run through the late thirties for each cohort. For another dozen years, until she is in her late forties, the typical mother has responsibility only for school-age children. A few more years, into her early fifties, and the last child forms a new family; this line is also plotted in Figure 1.

THE LONG TREND: DOWN, UP, DOWN

In the eighteenth century American women, pioneering in a new and bountiful nation, reproduced at very high rates. T. R. Malthus in his *Essay on Population* (first published in 1798) cited the United States growth rate as an illustration of the potential of natural increase if unfettered by positive or preventive checks.

The fertility experience of white American women during more than a century is portrayed in Figure 6. The cohorts of women born before 1850 bore nearly five children each. Fertility was already well below the eight-to-ten child average that may have prevailed in the eighteenth century, and it continued to decline among successive cohorts throughout the nineteenth century. Women born in the years 1900 to 1915 encountered the depression during some portion of their childbearing years, yet their replacement-level fertility rates seem less a response to the depression than a direct continuation of the long-term decline.

Fig. 6.   Fertility Measures for Birth Cohorts of White Women

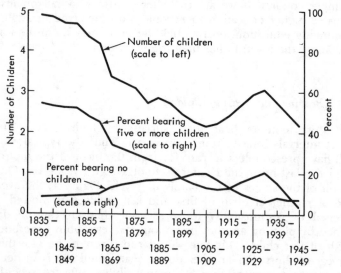

Data for the last three cohorts are estimates based on additional births expected according to a national sample survey.

When the children of the depression reached childbearing age they produced the "baby boom," which reached its peak among the cohorts of 1925-1939. The number of children born per woman reached only three at the height of the baby boom, a figure about the same as that experienced by the grandmothers of these women fifty years before and well below the reproductive levels of their great-grandmothers and earlier ancestors.

The subsequent "baby bust" (or baby dearth in the Census Bureau's more restrained terminology) dropped fertility rates down about as fast as they went up. The early childbearing behavior of the most recent cohorts, not included in Figure 6, reveals a further sharp drop to the lowest levels in our history. Whether the curve will drop farther, flatten out, or rise again is a topic of intense debate among demographers. Because the demographic profession has a record of having failed to foresee either the baby boom or the baby bust, we do not claim the right to impose on readers our own projections of future American fertility.

FAMILY SIZE AND THE BURDEN OF CHILD CARE

During the long fertility decline, the large family became less and less common. Among all cohorts of women born in this century fewer than one of every five women bore five or more children. Among the baby-boom mothers there was a modest resurgence of the large family, but much of the increased childbearing came about because many more women had two or three children rather than none or one. In the preceding and following generations of women, the two-child family was definitely the mode. Among younger women in a 1974 survey of childbearing attitudes and expectations, hardly any expected to have as many as four children and nearly three of every five expected to have exactly two.

Among the cohorts responsible for the depression baby bust, one distinctive pattern emerged that has not been followed before or since. As shown by the bottom line in Figure 6, there was a great increase in the number remaining childless. Among young women in the 1970s, who also plan very small families, fewer than ever expect to remain childless. Again we find evidence that marriage and a family that includes one's own children are nearly universal aspirations of young women entering adulthood in the late 1960s and early 1970s. The one-child family, which became a rarity during the baby boom, has reemerged in the thinking of a minority of contemporary young women as a reasonable goal. Whether many of these women will modify their goal after they have one child remains to be seen.

In light of the recent half-century of remarkable fluctuations in fertility rates, it is an unexpected feature of Figure 1 that all of the lines portraying the impact of fertility on the family life cycle are nearly flat (except for the earliest cohort). The increase in childbearing during the baby boom was accomplished largely by shortening the child-spacing intervals, and only to a small degree by extending the period of childbearing past age thirty or thirty-five.

The length of the childbearing and childrearing periods portrayed in Figure 1 did not expand much during the baby boom, but the burden of childbearing increased. Among married women living with spouse, about 18 percent in 1960 had both preschool and older children to care for. By 1973 this figure had dropped by one-third, to 12 percent.

Among married women living with spouse, some have not yet begun the family expansion years and many others in our low-mortality society have completed their childbearing duties and preside over what is called (with familistic bias) the empty nest. As a result of past and current changes in fertility rates and in the age distribution of women, the numbers and proportions of women without childrearing responsibilities increased during the 1960s. In 1960, two-thirds of married women with spouse present had no children under age eighteen living at home; the number of such women was twenty-nine million. In 1973 the corresponding number was thirty-five million and the proportion was nearly three-fourths. Demographic change reinforced cultural trends toward greater concern with female roles other than the care of children.

Participation in the Labor Force

During the twentieth century there have been fluctuations in most of those aspects of the life cycle that we have reviewed—especially in patterns of marriage and fertility. But whether age at marriage was rising or falling, whether fertility was rising or falling, whether the proportion of women with young children in the family was rising or falling, the proportion of women in the labor force was steadily rising. Among women of working age (defined as age fourteen and over), about one in five was in the labor force in 1900, about one in four in 1940, one in three in 1950, and nearly one in two in 1975.

EMPLOYMENT AND THE LIFE CYCLE

The rising rates of participation of women in the labor force are usually portrayed in snapshot rather than cohort terms. Thus in Chart 1A of Chapter 3 the participation rates of women in each age group are shown for four different years. These snapshot figures are an accurate portrayal of the aggregate experience, but as the authors point out, it is inappropriate to use data arranged in this way to make life cycle interpretations. In 1940, women in their early twenties had higher labor force participation rates than did women aged forty or fifty. But women who were young adults in 1940 reached age forty or fifty in the 1960s or 1970s, and their participation rates at that time are shown by the 1960 or 1974 lines in Chart 1A. Chart 1B of Chapter 3 is a graph of changing labor force participation rates for successive cohorts of women.

Although the official census practice was to define the working ages as beginning with age fourteen or sixteen, the development of nearly universal secondary schooling complicates interpretation of labor force participation rates at age below twenty. At ages above sixty interpretation is complicated by changing retirement patterns, patterns that are only imperfectly captured by census data.

The age profile of participation rates from age twenty to age sixty is flat for the cohort of women born in 1886-1895. Taking this cohort as a reference point, we see among subsequent cohorts two separate patterns of change, each of which has been remarkably persistent for more than half a century. One pattern is for each successive cohort of women to begin their working ages with greater participation rates. There are some irregularities in the hierarchical arrangement of the rates for the successive cohorts at younger ages, but a perfect ordering appears at all ages above thirty. The cohort of 1946-1955 demonstrates a great amount of increase at the early ages. This cohort also delayed marriage and sharply reduced childbearing.

The type of change in which each successive cohort begins a process with higher rates than the preceding cohort may be called generational change. A second type of change is indicated by a change in the shape of the age-curve for successive cohorts; this is life-cycle or career change. For labor force participation rates, career change is evident in the slant of the lines between ages forty and fifty. In a more detailed version of Chart 1B, the degree of upward tilt is greater for each successive cohort and is evident also at ages thirty to forty.

The career pattern of employment for the cohort of 1886-1895 conforms to the traditional pattern identified in Chapter 1. Before marriage and childbearing, a moderate proportion of women worked, but along with family responsibilities came permanent departure from the labor force for the vast majority of women. After children entered school, even after they grew up and left home, women stayed out of the labor market. It is this career pattern that has shifted with each succeeding cohort since that of 1886-1895. The dropoff in labor force participation as women move through the early stages of family formation and care for preschool children gradually diminished, so that for the cohorts of 1936-1945 and later, labor force participation at ages twenty-five to twenty-nine was nearly as great as at ages twenty to twenty-four. As women move into the later stages of family maturation, in which all of the children are in school and the oldest are leaving home, labor force participation rates rise from their minimum levels, and the amount of that rise has been increasing.

The continuation of both generational and career changes in labor force participation rates among so many successive cohorts defies any simple interpretation. The employment opportunities created by the economic boom of World War II and the military employment of men may have accelerated these changes, but the changes were evident before the war both in times of depression and in times of economic boom. The changes in participation rates persisted throughout periods of great fluctuation in familism—as indexed by marriage and fertility rates. The changes continued despite the steady decline throughout this period in the employment of women in domestic service (including employment to care for other women's children).

SCHOOLING, WORK, AND CHILDREN

The long-term increase in female labor force participation has not proceeded to the point where paid work for women is as universal as for men. Whether a woman works is related to her family status, childcare responsibilities, schooling, and other attributes.

Among women in the younger adult ages, continuing in school reduces labor force participation, although many women combine both activities. Data from the 1970 census show that at age eighteen, 37 percent of women attending school were also in the labor force, whereas 54 percent of those not in school were labor force participants. At age twenty-one, both figures were higher, 43 percent and 58 percent, respectively.

Acquisition of more education increases the likelihood of working after schooling is completed. Among women aged twenty-five to thirty-four in 1973, labor force participation rates increased from 42 percent for those who completed one to three years of high school, to 49 percent for high school graduates, 53 percent for those who completed one to three years of college, and 64 percent for those who graduated from college. Thus by the early 1970s, among women with some postsecondary education, working had become more common than remaining out of the labor force, even while these women were in the age range twenty-five to thirty-four during which nearly all were married and had young children.

Census data are available to permit calculation of labor force participation rates according to various attributes or combinations of attributes—age group, educational group, marital status group, etc. Each of the specified attributes has the expected effects, whatever the level of detailed classification by other attributes. For example, in 1970 among high school graduates age twenty-four, 88 percent of the never married women but 37 percent of those who were married and living with spouse were labor force participants. Among college graduates of the same age, 89 percent of the never married and 56 percent of married women, living with spouse, were in the labor force.

The long-term upward rise in labor force participation by women was accomplished in part by the shift of increasing proportions of the members of each successive cohort into the higher levels of educational attainment where working was more customary. But most of the upward rise in labor force participation rates occurred as a result of upward shifts in the specific rates for each category of age, education, and marital status.

To illustrate this pattern of upward shifts we shall consider another factor that has a strong effect on whether women seek paid employment, the presence of young children in the home. In Figure 7 labor force participation rates of married women, living with husband, are plotted for the years 1951 through 1972 for four groups: those whose youngest child is age six or over, those whose youngest child is aged three to five, those with a child under age three, and a composite of the last two groups. Each of the four lines in the graph has a sharp upward trend.

Fig. 7. Labor Force Participation Rates of Women Living with Spouse and Children

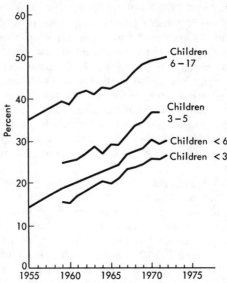

Figure 7 is based on a series of snapshots rather than a life-cycle format. Data are lacking for a true life-cycle portrait of changing labor force participation during the family formation, expansion, and shrinking phases. By piecing together data from a national survey taken in 1973 we can develop a partial illustration of how such a life-cycle portrait might look. Consider labor force participation rates for women of specified age, marital status, and age of youngest child in the home:

TABLE 2. LABOR FORCE PARTICIPATION RATES

	Never	Married—Spouse Present			
Age	*Married*	*No Children*	*Child under 3*	*Child 3-5*	*Child 6-17*
20-24	72	72	33	48	—*
25-34	86	77	—		54
35-44	78	60	—		53

Note: indicates not applicable or not available.

As a woman grows older, marries, has children, and her children grow older, she shifts from one category to another, either down a column, across a row, or diagonally down and right.

The status that has the most effect on labor force participation is the presence of very young children in the home. As the children grow out of infancy many women move back into the labor force, and as the children reach school age still more women take up paid employment. For several decades each new cohort of women has been displaying higher labor force participation rates at each life-cycle stage. Nevertheless, full-time maternal care of infants remains the predominant pattern. Even among the cohort of women born 1948-1953 (age twenty to twenty-four in 1973), two-thirds of those with infants at home were out of the labor force. Among men, nearly universal labor force participation prevails throughout all stages of the family life cycle, but among women, the family life cycle continues to be intimately bound up with the social and economic life cycles.

Variations and Other Themes*

We began with a simple sketch of the life cycle and showed how the timing of certain events had changed. The diminished force of mortality in middle age greatly augmented the likelihood of both partners in a marriage surviving past the age at which the youngest child leaves home and forms a new family. The diminished levels of fertility from the high rates prevailing in the eighteenth and early nineteenth centuries led to a pronounced concentration of the family expansion and child care stages of the typical life cycle within a narrow age range. Trends in education, fluctuations in the typical age at marriage, and large swings in levels of fertility were also assessed for their effects on the typical female social life cycle. By the time we introduced explicit consideration of rates of participation in the labor force, the analysis became rather complex, for each of the attributes and processes affects all of the others. Even if all of the desired life-cycle data were available to us, so that we did not have to rely so much upon potentially misleading inferences from snapshot data, the descriptive task would still be enormously complex. We have been compelled to present illustrative results rather than full tabulations. In our attempts to retain simplicity in the face of enormous complexity, we have glossed over a number of complications and stressed only the main themes. Let us take note of some of these complications.

MOTHER-CHILD FAMILIES

The basic life-cycle chart (Figure 1) assumes a simple sequence from birth to marriage to childbearing to childrearing to death of spouse. In fact, not all childbearing is confined to marriage nor do all marriages endure until one spouse dies. According to the best estimates, approximately one-fifth of all women marrying in the late 1950s and early 1960s were pregnant at the time of their first marriage. An additional 5 percent had borne a child prior to marriage. Premarital pregnancy and childbearing within the first year of marriage have been shown to be associated (though imperfectly) with higher rates of marital disruption and lower economic achievement of husbands.

More common than premarital and extramarital childbearing are premarital and extramarital sexual relations. With the recent spread of highly effective contraceptive technology and the augmented availability of abortion as a remedy for contraceptive failure, childbearing outside of marriage may become less frequent. But the future may bring changes in lifestyle that will lead to deliberate change in this pattern; hence a more precise forecast would refer to a reduction in the bearing of unwanted children outside of marriage.

Also important as a social issue and as a complication of our simple life-cycle portrait is childrearing outside of marriage. Widowhood in the early years of the family life cycle has become rare, but separation and divorce are distinctly commonplace. Absence of husband may be a prelude to divorce or it may represent a temporary arrangement. The prevalence of absent spouses has fluctuated widely, reaching its peak during World War II. Divorce rates have also fluctuated widely, and in the early 1970s were zooming upward after a long decline from the post-World War II peak.

Absence of a husband is, of course, a spur to labor force participation by the wife, even if young children are present. For illustration, the patterns for 1973, presented above for women in several groups according to age, marital status, and presence of children, can be expanded to include women who were separated, divorced, or otherwise living apart from spouse. At ages twenty-five to thirty-four, the spouse-absent women with no children had a labor force participation rate of 81 percent, whereas those with school-age children had a rate of 70 percent. Both rates are higher than for the women who were living with spouse, and the difference is especially large for women with children.

RETIREMENT AND MIGRATION

We have paid more attention to the early stages of the family life cycle than to the later stages. There has been little study of the patterns of retirement from the labor force by women, although the topic is of rapidly increasing social and political importance. As each successive cohort of women reaches retirement age increasing proportions will have been in the labor force through most of their adult years. Growing proportions will qualify for Social Security or other pensions on the basis of their own work careers. Because men die at younger ages than do women and are typically the older partner in a marriage, widows far outnumber widowers. This sex differential in marital status at the older ages is aggravated by the much greater remarriage probabilities for widowers than for widows.

At most ages there is little of the residential segregation by sex that is so common by race, ethnicity, and economic status. But to the extent that older persons tend to relocate, whether to retirement centers or to nursing homes and other special housing, an unusual degree of sex segregation occurs. At younger ages there is a moderate degree of sex segregation during the period after schooling and before marriage. Cities with a rapidly growing clerical labor force—Washington, D.C., for example—tend to attract more young women than young men, and the imbalance may be sufficient to affect probabilities and ages of marriage and remarriage. An analogous concentration of young men is found in mining towns and manufacturing centers. For example, the surge of persons to Alaska in the mid-1970s for employment in pipeline construction was heavily male.

DISPERSION AROUND THE AVERAGE

Most of the charts and data we have presented utilize averages. Around any average there is a range of variation. Among women in the cohort born 1910 to 1919 who eventually married and bore children, the median age at first marriage was 21.7 years. One-fourth of these women married by the time they were 18.8 years. Three-fourths had married by age 25.2. The graphic portrayal of the typical life cycle in Figure 1 and our discussion of typical ages conceal this large variance. Few members of a cohort actually follow the typical pattern. The average and the typical are statistical constructs useful for summarizing and generalizing, but they are as hard to find in the real world as is the "average woman with 2.2 children." In a fuller description and analysis of trends it would be necessary to consider ranges and variation. In assessing the decline in average expected family size from above three to about two children, for example, it is highly informative to know also that the zero and one-child families did not acquire many new converts. Rather there was a marked increase in the proportion of women choosing the two-child family rather than the three or four-child family.

INTERLOCKING SYSTEMS OF CAUSES AND EFFECTS

The various events in the family and social life cycles are interlocking. Causes and effects are often intermingled and a single trend may be both cause and effect. An especially intriguing demographic example pertains to the causes and effects of cohort size. Completion of schooling, entry into the labor force, marriage, and the beginning of childbearing all tend to occur while women are within the age range eighteen to twenty-four years. The number of women aged eighteen to twenty-four in a given year is determined almost entirely by the number of girls born eighteen to twenty-four years earlier; mortality and immigration may be ignored for our purposes. The number of girls born in a year depends on the number of women in the reproductive ages and on birth rates. The size of successive generations is affected both by size of the previous generation and by the trend in fertility.

The number of women aged eighteen to twenty-four, and hence the number actively engaged in the various life cycle changes that are concentrated in early adulthood, has fluctuated widely during the recent decades of great social change. From past census data and simple projections the trend in numbers of women aged eighteen to twenty-four is as follows (numbers in millions): 1910, 6.3; 1930, 7.9; 1950, 8.1; 1960, 8.0; 1970, 12.2; 1980, 14.6; 1990, 12.3. Because of low fertility early in the 1920s and 1930s, the size of the successive cohorts of women reaching adulthood was rather stable during World War II. It was during this period that a concerted effort was made to increase female labor force participation. A few years later during the postwar economic expansion birth rates rose rapidly. Between 1960 and 1970 the number of women aged eighteen to twenty-four rose by more than half. Any knowledgeable forecaster trying in 1960 to assess whether the rapid increase in female labor force participation of the previous two decades would continue for the next two would undoubtedly have been skeptical. The prognosticator would note that the economy during the 1960s was faced with absorbing the burgeoning number of new male entrants each year (as a result of the baby boom of the late 1940s) and that it would be extraordinarily difficult simultaneously to expand the labor market rapidly enough to accommodate the burgeoning number of young women. Yet this is precisely what happened.

The fact that increasing proportions of these young women were finding jobs meant that the size of the young female labor force was increasing far more rapidly than the rate of 50 percent in ten years that was true of the size of the total cohort. Such a rapid expansion of labor supply must, according to simple economic theory, have tended to reduce the rates of job advancement, of wage raises, and of confidence of these workers in their career outlook. In any case, it is the women in these very large cohorts who have postponed marriage until a year or so later in the life cycle, have postponed and greatly reduced childbearing, have cut back sharply on the size of family they see as desirable, and have stirred political controversy over the status and rights of women.

There is no way for social scientists to specify precisely the causes of these various changes, or even to determine to what extent addititudinal changes affect later behavior and to what extent it is the behavioral changes that affect the attitudinal changes. Social scientists looking forward to the 1980s, when cohort sizes will for the first time be falling sharply, differ in their judgment of whether there will be a new resurgence of familism with a lowered age at marriage and increased childbearing.

VARIATIONS

By keeping our discussion focused on trends in the timing of events in the life cycle, we have deliberately ignored a whole range of differences among women that cause them to differ in the way their lives are ordered. One set of differences is composed of those variations in personality, biology, and other aspects of individuality that lead to differentiation in the sequencing of life-cycle events. Another set of differences, overlapping with the first, is the divergent social settings in which people are raised and which affect their perceptions of the world around them, the opportunities open to them, and the behavior expected of them. Race, social class, and geographic location (the South, ghetto, suburb) are among the most readily measured attributes that typically correlate (albeit imperfectly) with these divergent social settings. Our discussion has touched occasionally on variation among women of varying social and economic attributes. But we have eschewed fuller treatment of the dimensions of variation in life-cycle patterns. It is essential in assessing the role of women in changing the economy and the role of the economy in changing women to be aware of differences among Negroes, Spanish Americans, American Indians, and white Catholics of Irish descent who live in South Boston. Within and between these groups there is variation patterned by the educational and occupational levels of one's parents and oneself and by the income and wealth of one's family of origin and one's family of procreation.

Social scientists have not even begun to study the life cycle of women with this degree of social perspective. Without knowledge of the patterned variation among women in the structure of their life cycles, it is risky indeed to try to foretell the future, even a few years ahead. We have made a few broad and general extrapolations of some of the strongest past trends, but a series of more specific predictions would not be justified. What is justified is a skepticism concerning simple causal assessments and a scientific bewilderment at the complexity of human experience. Generalizations and conclusions we leave to those of Shakespearean vision.

Juanita M. Kreps and R. John Leaper

3

Home Work, Market Work, and the Allocation of Time

The allocation of work within the family has been traced by Galbraith back to the era when ". . . the man did the heavier field work or the more heroic tasks of the hunt or predation; the woman managed the poultry and made clothes." In that stage of history, physical strength was a major factor in determining who performed which productive tasks.

With industrialization and urbanization, the pattern of males working outside and females inside the home came to be translated into males' market and females' nonmarket work, with men moving into jobs that commanded wages. Labor market activity of men thus called for specific working hours and rates of pay, and introduced arrangements that required equally explicit exchanges of money. Nonmarket activity for women, by contrast, came to be characterized by irregular and unspecified working periods, consumption of production without monetary exchange or valuation, and often the consumption of production by the producer herself. The fact that the female's work did not enter the market meant that her working time could be less precisely defined than the male's, and further that no estimation of the value of the female's services needed to be made.

R. JOHN LEAPER *is a director in the Department of Labor and Immigration of the Australian Public Service. Dr. Leaper was a Senior Tutor in the Department of Economics at the University of Melbourne and was co-author, with Professor Kreps, of a chapter in* The Manpower Report of the President, *April 1975.*

In the marketplace, decisions involving allocation are made on the basis of relative prices and utilities. By comparing the wages offered, a worker can choose between offering his labor or not offering it and consuming leisure instead. Also, he can choose between various work and pay alternatives. However, a woman's decision as to how to allocate her time is more complicated. She and her family must make a three-way decision: how much of her time to give to home work without dollar compensation, how much to market work for pay, and how much to leisure. The absence of monetary measures of the value of home services means that she must impute some value to that work before deciding whether her working time is better spent in the home or in the marketplace. The value of her leisure time, too, is obscure; since her time in home work receives no dollar value, how does she reckon the cost of not working when at home?

Economic development signals changes in the types of productive activity demanded. Education has replaced strength as a major determinant of who performs which tasks; and other developments have enhanced the abilities of women to compete in the production of market goods and services, thereby shifting some of the roles observed in earlier periods. Nevertheless, differences persist between the employee whose services carry a price tag, enabling him to evaluate work alternatives and working hours with reference to prices determined in the market, and the worker whose tasks have no specific dollar worth. Women continue to perform most of the latter jobs, and men most of the former.

Until recently both social and economic factors continued to limit women's market roles. Education for women has been geared to nonmarket work and to a narrow range of career options. Since most of what the woman has traditionally produced has received no payment at all, the monetary value of her productive capacities has been considered small and her alternatives historically limited. Moreover, as their market work options have improved, their leisure options have become even more limited; home work continues to demand the time left over from market jobs.

Women's Market Work: Recent Changes

In the early stages of industrialization, the division of work roles that developed was not inappropriate. Wages and productivity were low by today's standards; long working days were required even to insure a subsistence level of living. After farming, manufacturing became the major productive activity, and physical strength was often a major requisite. Families were large, and the technology of production in the home primitive. The time women spent on essential nonmarket activities left little room for choice between work or leisure. Given these circumstances, it is not surprising that market work for a woman at the turn of the century was limited to the period between education and marriage or at the latest, the birth of the first child. A female's life expectancy was less than fifty years, and when she survived to fifty she had likely produced six children. Soon after marrying, she left the labor market permanently and had responsibility for young children most of the rest of her life. Only one out of every five women over fourteen years old was engaged in any market activities. In 1900 the working woman was young and single.

Today, two out of every three working women are married. Nearly half of all women over sixteen years of age are in the labor market. Female life expectancy at birth is now over seventy-five years and average family size is barely two children. While married women may drop out of the work force with the birth of the first child, an ever growing proportion later return to the labor market. Women now have market worklives that are only slightly shorter than those of men.

Recent changes in women's working patterns can be explained by several major factors: the events associated with the Second World War, a growth in the services sector of the economy, improvements in household technology, and reductions in family size.

THE INFLUENCE OF THE SECOND WORLD WAR

Immense social upheaval was wrought during the Second World War, but even greater changes occurred in the period which followed, since an evolution in women's work has been underway for some time. Between 1900 and 1940, the proportion of American women over fourteen years of age engaged in market activities rose from one in five to one in four. Married women became more important to the labor force, but single women were the major source of female labor. Nearly half the working women were single, and nearly one third of the remainder were widowed, divorced, or separated.

The requirements of an industrial economy at war quickly

changed these proportions as patriotism and pay induced women to assume jobs formerly held only by men. Within five years, over one third of all women were in the work force, nearly half of them married. Despite several deterrents—the returning veterans' displacement of many women from the jobs they had temporarily filled; the sudden rise in family size; the fears of postwar recessions and widespread unemployment—women continued to seek market work. In the succeeding three decades, they entered the labor market in proportions that dwarfed their wartime involvement.

THE GROWTH IN SERVICES

Postwar growth in the number of women in the work force was due in part to growth in the number of jobs women had traditionally performed. Although the trend toward service production had begun earlier (in the quarter-century before the war, employment in the service-producing sector rose by 57 percent while employment in the goods-producing sector rose only 37 percent), the growth in services subsequently became even more dramatic. Goods-producing employment increased another third, while service-producing employment more than doubled in the quarter-century following the war. This trend has continued. During the 1970s, employment in the service sector has risen steadily at around 3 percent each year, but employment in the goods sector has shown no net growth.

For the female worker, this shift has been highly significant. Much of the growth in the service sector either has been in areas traditionally designated as women's work, or has utilized skills usually thought to be those of women. For example, education and health have been two of the fastest growing areas. Since teaching children and caring for the sick were by custom the domain of female activity, the jobs that were expanding were those for which employers sought women. A third area of rapid growth was clerical services. Although a relatively new source of employment that was foreign to the precise skills utilized in domestic female activity, clerical services nevertheless demanded the type of manual dexterity and patience expected of women in the home.

IMPROVEMENTS IN HOUSEHOLD TECHNOLOGY

Technology came to the home as well as the marketplace during the postwar period. Gadgetry became common throughout the range of domestic activities, with new products introduced to ease the time and effort required for most household chores. With greatly improved efficiency in their nonmarket work, large numbers of women were able to manage their households in a fraction of the time formerly required. Different responses to this growth in time free of household work became apparent. Some women spent their time achieving small marginal increases in household production, or gave increasing attention to child care. Others, for whom market work remained outside the range of choice, found an alternative type of nonmarket activity increasingly important: volunteer community work by women grew dramatically. For still others, the options included alternative work in those market opportunities that were increasingly available to women in the postwar American economy.

FAMILY SIZE

During the decades of the fifties and sixties, improvements in household technology gave women greater control over their time than they had ever enjoyed. This greater freedom was augmented by a resumption of the long-term decline in fertility which had accompanied urbanization early in the century but temporarily had been reversed during the immediate postwar era. Since the care of young children traditionally has been the most important constraint on women's market activities, reduction in the number of children born to a woman reduces the portion of her lifespan devoted to child rearing. Moreover, technology not only assisted in a reduction in the number of children born to each woman, thereby reducing the length of time she was responsible for the young; it also made it possible for her to plan the timing and spacing of births to coincide with her career interests.

Whereas a woman in the first quarter of this century might have had six children over an extended period which often ended only shortly before her death, the woman of the last quarter is likely to have only two children, and her childbearing years will be completed in perhaps the first third of her lifespan. These lengthened periods in which women have no young dependents offer options for market work or other uses of time never before available to women and their families.

Women's Market Work: The Scene Today

In summary, the demand for female labor skills, dramatized during the Second World War and continued in the wake of growth in the service sector of the postwar economy, has been met by women who have reduced the time spent on household management and child care. Married women provided two-thirds of the 17.5 million women workers who doubled the size of the female labor force in the United States in the third quarter of the twentieth century. Over two-thirds of all American women over age eighteen are currently married with husbands present. In 1950, less than a quarter of the women so classified were in the labor force; by 1974, the proportion had reached 43 percent and was still rising.

Of the important variables influencing married women's labor force activity—age, education, marital status, presence of children, husband's income—age appears to be the most significant overall, when the data are shown cross-sectionally (*e.g.,* for 1974). From Table 1 and Chart 1A it can be seen that few older women were in the labor force in the prewar period; the proportion working outside the home declined steadily for age groups beyond the mid-twenties. By 1950, however, women aged thirty-five and over were in the market in large numbers and in subsequent decades the proportions have risen strikingly.

TABLE 1. LABOR FORCE PARTICIPATION RATES* OF WOMEN, BY AGE GROUPS, SELECTED YEARS, UNITED STATES, 1950 TO 1974

Age Group	1950	1960	1970	1974
16 and 17 years	30.1	29.1	34.9	40.4
18 and 19 years	51.3	51.1	53.7	58.3
20 to 24 years	46.1	46.2	57.8	63.2
25 to 34 years	34.0	36.0	45.0	52.4
35 to 44 years	39.1	43.5	51.1	54.7
45 to 54 years	38.0	49.8	54.4	54.6
55 to 64 years	27.0	37.2	43.0	40.7
65 years and over	9.7	10.8	9.7	8.2
Total 16 years and over	33.9	37.8	43.4	45.7

Source: Manpower Report of the President, April 1975.
*Percent of noninstitutional population in the labor force

The shifts in women's market work activity depicted in Chart 1A mirror several influences, including the effect of fertility changes on women's workforce participation. In 1940 the U.S. crude birth rate was 19.4 children per thousand of population.

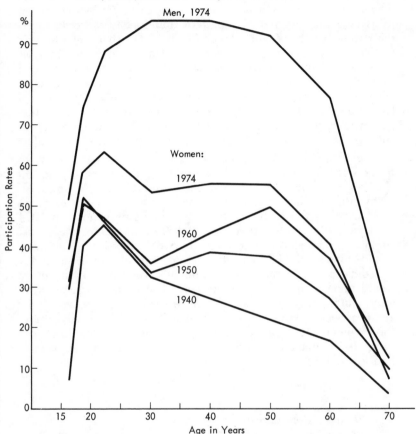

Chart 1A. *Labor Force Participation Rates by Age for Women in 1940, 1950, 1960, and 1974—and for Men in 1974*

Sources: U.S. Bureau of the Census, *Census of the United States 1940* and U.S. Department of Labor, *Manpower Report of the President,* April 1975

By 1955 it had risen to the highest level in three decades, 25.0 per thousand. This postwar "baby boom" severely restricted the work force activity of women in the childbearing group, aged twenty to thirty-four, whereas the participation of older women was gaining in the decade of the 1950s.

However, the long-term decline in fertility resumed, and by 1965 the birth rate had returned to its prewar level of 19.4. This decline continued into the seventies until by 1975 it stood at less than 15.0—the lowest in the nation's history. The 1960s and 1970s have also seen especially large increases in workforce participation by younger women, as the worklives for women begin to assume the inverted "U" pattern traditionally associated with the pattern for men. Indeed, the familiar "M" shape of women's worklives depicted by the cross-sectional data shown in Chart 1A does not fit the pattern demonstrated by a cohort of women when traced through the lifetime (see Chart 1B). The cohorts of women born between 1916 and 1935, who were the mothers of large numbers of postwar babies, did show a reduction in participation rates during their childbearing years. But the more recent cohorts display rising participation rates during that stage of life.

Predicting future participation rates for today's twenty to thirty-four year olds is hazardous in the light of recent significant changes in fertility and in women's attitudes toward work. Already, the official projections of women's work rates made in 1973 have proved to be far too low, with some cohorts in 1974 surpassing the rates expected for 1990. Less conservative assumptions, based on cohort trends over the last two decades, would suggest worklife patterns such as those shown in Chart 1B.

Estimates of the duration of women's worklives in the future would seem to indicate at least twenty-five years of market work after childrearing, with an overall worklife that averages only about a decade less than that of men. In market activity, therefore, women are approaching patterns similar to those men observe. In nonmarket work, however, no such similarity appears to be forthcoming.

Women's Dual Careers

Throughout three quarters of a century of women's rapid movement into market activities, their responsibility for home work has changed very little. Improvements in technology and reduced family size have lowered the time necessary to manage a household, but the amount of time necessary for such duties is by no means trivial. The social convention that it is a woman's responsibility—many would say her primary responsibility—to manage and maintain the household continues to exercise a severe constraint on her choice of market activity.

Chart 1B. *Cohort Labor Force Participation: Men Born 1906-1915; Women Born 1886-1975*

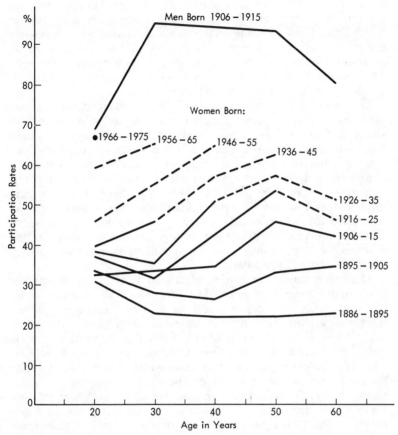

Sources: Economic Report of the President (Washington, D.C.: Government Printing Office, 1973). Projections to 1990 by the authors, based on linear extrapolation of 1957-1974 data.

For many women, particularly those unable to afford the gadgetry required to increase the efficiency of household production or to reduce the costs of child care, or those who are unable to locate market work with the earnings or hours necessary to cover such costs, nonmarket obligations preclude any sort of market activity. For the woman who is able to take on market work, the paid job is an additional occupation which, when combined with home work, means that she is pursuing a "dual" career. Only by a careful allocation of time can a woman with children manage both market and nonmarket production, particularly if the former is full-time. Less than one in ten married women who work hold down full-time jobs for the whole year. Three quarters are in part-time employment, and half of these for only part of the year. The remainder of the working married women take on full-time employment, but for only a fraction of the year.

The term "duel" careers may well be more appropriate, as the time and effort required for full-time market jobs come into sharp conflict with the demands placed by home responsibilities. Since women are expected to produce nonmarket goods and services whether or not they are engaged in market employment, it is easy to understand why women choose jobs that are part-time or part-year. Coincidentally, these work schedules of women have meshed with industry's needs; much of the service sector growth has called for only part-time or part-year employment. Thus, the pattern of economic development was such as to allow for the entrance of large numbers of women to market work, much of which was on a limited basis.

The value which the market places on women's skills has not been high. Instead of improving their work alternatives to include all types of work, women have been stereotyped in the marketplace, just as they have been stereotyped in their home work. More than one third of the married women in the workforce are clerical workers. One fifth are service workers. One sixth are professionals, and one sixth are operatives. Most of the remainder are in the retail trade. The working woman is a typist, maid, teacher, nurse, cashier, or saleswoman (see Chart 2). Few women participate in craft or kindred occupations; few find employment as professionals in engineering, law, or medicine. Within the industries where women do find employment, they are on the lower rungs of the occupational ladder. Despite their education, women have failed to make significant inroads into the most valuable market occupations.

Women have been hampered in their choice of occupation not by the level, but by the type of education they receive. Indeed, women have had impressive levels of educational attainment which, until recently, men have not matched. In 1952, the average number of years of school completed by all men in the work-

Chart 2. *Sex Composition of Industry Groups and the Distribution of Women Workers*

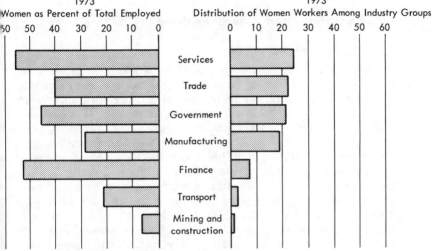

Source: *Manpower Report of the President,* April 1975.

force was 10.4; the average for women was 12.0. Not until 1974 did the educational attainment of men catch up to that of women in the workforce, at 12.5 years each.

But on entering the work force most women have had to rely on the vocational training they had in high school. Apart from training for nonmarket activities through courses such as home economics, women have been encouraged to concentrate on learning the market skills of shorthand and typing. Their market careers have been viewed as temporary, covering a short period in the workforce before their children are born. Little thought has been given to that significant period of a woman's labor force activity in the quarter century or more after children have reached school age. Even when post-high school vocational training has been undertaken by women, it has followed closely the traditional patterns of sex segregation. Ninety-five percent of the health and 79 percent of business and commercial courses in vocational and technical schools are taken by women. Ninety-eight percent of technical, industrial, and trade subjects are taken by men. Without a range of education and training programs leading to different vocations, women will continue to face similar occupational limitations.

Three-way Time Allocation:
Home Work, Market Work, and Leisure

THE VALUE OF NONMARKET WORK

Work done in the home, primarily by women, obviously contributes to the welfare of families and the society. An economic appraisal of this work is difficult, however, since no dollar value is imputed to work done outside the marketplace. When a wife shifts from home to market work, it is generally assumed that her earnings improve the family's economic well-being; accordingly, the national income accounts show that the Gross National Product is increased by the amount of her earnings. But the family's gains from the additional market work might be revealed as illusory if precise estimates were available. The gains are illusory if work is undertaken purely for increased income which, although apparently forthcoming, is actually offset when costs of foregone services are imputed. The costs of foregone earnings plus work-related costs may actually exceed the money increase in earnings, resulting in a decline in real income when the wife moves into the labor force.

The assumption that a family can quickly discern the net economic effects of such a shift is not necessarily warranted for two reasons: 1) there is no way to estimate the costs of the services foregone when the wife goes from home to marketplace; and, 2) many of the services performed in the home may have less value to the family than additional income, and yet the cost of having a nonfamily member do them could be greater than the wife's market earnings. The fact that the market price for domestic services exceeds the value imputed to such services in some homes explains why wives leave their home work undone and perform the same services for pay. The lower the family income, the greater the need for additional earnings and the lower the imputed value of home work, including child care.

Confusion as to whether a movement from home to market work contributes to societal welfare is compounded by national income accounting, which increases the national product when services are provided through the market but not when the same services are performed in the home. The fact that labor done in the marketplace, but not that carried on in the home, is rewarded by pay which presumably bears some relation to its value makes it difficult to calculate the net gain from women's growing contribution to market work. However, the important consideration is not the failure to measure the value of home work but the tendency to impute a low market value to those services which, being customarily performed in the home, have commanded no price at all. Cleaning, laundry, and cooking have brought low wages in the labor market, reflecting the fact that in most instances these services bear no price tags. Not only has the buyer been conditioned to view these services as cheap; the women who do the work are conditioned to think of them in the same way. Are they not free services in the home?

THE VALUE OF MARKET WORK

The low value imputed to women's domestic work may help to explain the similarly low appraisal of the work she does for pay. From the "free" services offered in the home, low-priced services in the labor market called for only a comfortably short step. Any work done by a woman came to be regarded as of less value than that done by a man. The narrow range of jobs available to women, moreover, has led frequently to conditions of oversupply and a pushing down of wages paid for "female" jobs. The limitations on market work set by the demands of dual careers reinforce the traditional view of women's work. Although education, job experience, and level of responsibility are ready explanations for lower female productivity and hence lower pay, it is difficult to separate cause from effect when analyzing sex differences in earnings.

Even with the growing attachment of women to the work force, a substantial difference in male-female earnings remains. Part-time employment reduces average female earnings, but even when allowance is made for this, female earnings fall well short of those of males. Currently, median earnings of year-round full-time women workers are only 58 percent those of men, having fallen from 64 percent two decades ago. Attempts to explain the earnings gap between men and women have been made by adjusting for such factors as occupation, education, and work experience. Various studies have produced remaining "unexplained" differences in earnings of approximately one-third. There is a strong implication that this remaining difference in earnings is the result of sex discrimination and that even further differences in earnings are the result of role differentiation based on sex rather than the requirements of individual occupations. Both of these factors therefore result in low values being placed on women's market work.

THE VALUE OF LEISURE TIME

The loss of free time has seldom been protested by married women when they enter the labor market; indeed, they have seemed eager to demonstrate that they can manage both home and market work without making heavy demands on the rest of the family. This position is understandable, given the traditional view that women should stay in the home, which has led them to feel they had to justify any assumption of market work. Yet in the allocation of time between market and nonmarket work, the value of the third dimension of choice—free time—has received little explicit consideration. Economic analysis has valued free time in terms of the market earnings foregone by the consumption of leisure. When the work/leisure choice is simply one of market work or leisure, this valuation may be sufficient. But when the work/leisure choice is one of three alternatives, with two of them carrying no explicit prices, the opportunity-cost approach becomes more difficult and for women, whose market and nonmarket values may be understated, the analysis has limited usefulness.

Studies of family time allocation before and after women have taken market jobs have revealed different patterns of redistribution. An increase in the amount of market work done by the adult members of a family may be accompanied by some reduction in the amount and quality of home services, but it appears that working wives and their families continue to perform most of their own household work. The big tradeoff for the woman's market work is not a reduction in her home work, but a reduction in her free time. In one study, the total workload for the wife rose by an average of thirteen hours per week as a result of her move into market work, while that of her husband actually dropped by an average of 1.5 hours per week. Clearly, women are not gaining greater leisure from the higher family income attained as a result of their market jobs, although such an increase would be predicted from the economist's work/leisure model.

Alternative Allocations of Time

FULL-TIME MARKET WORK

One of the major explanations for the lack of male involvement in home work has been the widely accepted practice of packaging market work in eight-hour days and five-day weeks. Such workweeks, when added to commuting time and other work-related duties, make the market work commitment extremely time consuming. The prevalence of part-time work among working wives attests to the need for a reexamination of working hours. Over two-thirds of all part-time workers are women and three-fifths of them are married. The two industry groups dominated by women—the finance and service industries—employ nearly half of all part-time workers.

With a continued growth of the service sector of the economy, part-time work is likely to increase. In addition, the length of the full-time work package will probably continue to decline, narrowing the difference between full-time and part-time employment. In some instances forty-hour workweeks have been compressed into four or even three days instead of the usual five. Surprisingly, many women have found these arrangements advantageous since they allow much of the nonmarket production to be done in three-day weekends. A more promising suggestion for the long-term reallocation of work roles and time, however, appears to be an approach which has been called "flexitime." Rather than compressing the workweek, it would extend the period of time during which the usual full-time workload could be completed. Workers could choose within a given range of starting and finishing times, as long as they were present during a short period of "core" time each day, and as long as they completed a set number of hours within a given time period—usually a month.

If such arrangements came to be widespread, it would be possible for male workers to take on increased responsibility for nonmarket production which often involves irregular hours and sometimes conflicts with full-time market schedules. In a period when the level of economic activity is expected to slow, some rescheduling of work would be particularly appropriate. Work-sharing arrangements could further redefine full-time work responsibilities and enable both men and women to participate in market activities without necessitating reductions in either nonmarket production or leisure time. Temporary work force withdrawals may also offer new sources of flexibility. To current practices such as postponed labor force entry, extended vacations, leave-without-pay, and early retirements, which have changed male worklives dramatically, it would be possible, for example, to add maternity and paternity leaves. Arrangements for phasing in and out of full-time work, or assuming a reduced workload permanently, would open possibilities for improvements in time allocation and ultimately in the quality of life available to American families.

CHILD CARE

Family responsibilities, particularly child care responsibilities, are still a dominant influence on women's work roles. As Table 2 shows, the presence of young children lowers participation rates for women significantly. Older children now have less effect on women's market work; and participation rates for married women with children six to seventeen years are higher than those of married women with no children—a difference that reflects the higher work rates of younger women, even when they have children under the age of eighteen.

TABLE 2. LABOR FORCE PARTICIPATION RATES OF MARRIED WOMEN, HUSBAND PRESENT, BY PRESENCE AND AGE OF CHILDREN, UNITED STATES, 1950 TO 1974

Year	Total	No Children under 18	Children 16-17 only	Children under 6 years	
				and 6-17	without 6-17
1950	23.8	30.3	28.3	12.6	11.2
1960	30.5	34.7	39.0	18.9	18.2
1970	40.8	42.2	49.2	30.5	30.2
1974	43.0	43.0	51.2	32.9	35.7

Source: Manpower Report of the President, April 1975

The impact of childrearing on female participation rates would lessen if the availability and cost of child care facilities were significantly improved. Day care centers, nursery schools, and similar group facilities now accommodate fewer than one out of every ten children of working mothers. Care in private homes by relatives or nonrelatives, often in pooled neighborhood arrangements, accounts for 90 percent of child care. Black working mothers rely more heavily on relatives than white women; six out of every ten children of black working women, and four out of every ten children of white working women, are being cared for this way. Reliance on relatives is essential, since many working women cannot afford to pay for day care. About half of relatives who care for children provide the service free.

There is a trend toward greater provision of group care services, especially in large urban centers. Between 1965 and 1973, licensed day care facilities more than doubled their capacity, and a survey revealed that women in New York City used this type of child care twice as often as women in the nation as a whole. But even with recent growth, current day care facilities could accommodate only one out of every six children of working mothers, assuming no use of the centers by nonworking women.

Female work force participation rates have risen fastest in recent years for women with the greatest child care needs—mothers of children under six years of age, even those with children under three years of age. With the need for child care rising rapidly and the use of group facilities becoming more widespread, a case can be made for close governmental supervision of the establishment and quality of child care centers. Provision for day care facilities by business firms is also gaining in popularity. Increased use of group day care arrangements by both working mothers and fathers will likely increase with the continued increase in labor force activity of young women, although the decline in numbers of births will mean that there will be fewer children overall in the home or the day care center.

SEX PREFERENCES FOR NONMARKET WORK ROLES

Family decisions as to the performance of nonmarket tasks—long set by social custom—are now becoming conscious choices within family units. Who should do what, how much of it should be done, and how much value accrues from the production of nonmarket goods and services, are decisions open to the family. In the light of recent changes in family size and the growing acceptance of women in market jobs, some reexamination of work roles would seem inevitable. Work preferences of males and females may undergo rapid change. Increasing use of group care for young children, greater reliance on the market to produce many of the goods and services formerly performed in the home, and a wider range of job options for women should encourage greater flexibility in the work choices of men as well as women.

Men will continue to face a conflict between the need to meet the obligations of their jobs and a possible preference for spending additional time in home work. Women have faced this conflict increasingly as they have taken on more demanding and satisfying market roles, and have continued to consider nonmarket work as their own responsibility. Men have avoided nonmarket work, not only because home work has been traditionally done by women, but also because these tasks have been regarded as demeaning to men. Laundry, household cleaning, and other nonmarket jobs performed by women were beneath the male dignity. Indeed, men performing "women's work" brought derisive comments, revealing the social unacceptability of such an allocation of nonmarket work.

These attitudes appear to be changing. Women's successes in the marketplace have set a trend that is not likely to come to an abrupt halt. They will continue to ask for more responsible market work and will not be able to maintain home work at traditional levels. Improvements in household technology and productivity can postpone the reallocation of nonmarket roles, but the time-intensive nature of domestic activities suggests that such a postponement is temporary. Just as men will eventually assume a greater share of nonmarket responsibilities, regardless of traditional patterns of work roles and social acceptability, women will no longer assume that they alone are to provide home services. The new division of labor, although slow to emerge, offers far wider lifestyle options to both sexes.

LABOR FORCE MOBILITY AND ATTACHMENT

The growing preference of women for careers may begin to affect a family's location as well as its division of time. With a more permanent attachment to the labor force, the woman's job will have to be considered when decisions on family location are made. Whereas the family's geographical mobility has in the past been associated with job changes of the male household head, the pattern will need to be modified to take account of two market careers. Both families and firms will need to reevaluate the extent to which families are able to relocate in the course of the parents' worklives.

Relocation brought about by the needs of the husband's career has been a major factor underlying the intermittent workforce participation of women, and has contributed to the higher rates of unemployment experienced by women. Their stronger attachment to the labor market may narrow the male-female unemployment differential in the long run. But it may also temporarily raise the differential, if women who currently withdraw from the labor market—rather than prolong a job search in times of high unemployment—persist in their attempts to locate market work. The most recent statistics on female unemployment suggest that the latter change in attitudes and attachment is currently occurring.

Attitudes and Expectations

Nostalgia for early twentieth century America, whose rural settings spawned large families in which mothers worked tirelessly but never outside their homes, continues to surface. Expectations forged in that era are not easy to set aside, although today's scene is strikingly different in many dimensions: families are small and one-generational; life is fast-paced, crowded and urban; educational levels of both parents and children are much higher. Women's domestic roles that served families so well in that earlier stage are no longer appropriate. Yet the stereotype lingers. During the last quarter of this century woman's commitment to market work, until recently limited in duration and significance, will likely be as strong as a man's. And although she will continue to perform domestic duties, she will also assume a wide variety of market jobs, including the highly specialized, the technical, the most demanding and the most satisfying. Along the way, however, a second stereotype has appeared. Appropriate market jobs for women, the conventional wisdom holds, are those fashioned from skills formerly learned in the home. Women workers are thus heavily concentrated in a few areas: elementary and secondary teaching, nursing, domestic and other services, clerical and sales jobs that call for meticulous care and patience. Some of these jobs are held almost exclusively by women. Indeed, the growing demand for clerical, sales, and service personnel could not have been met except by drawing on nonworking women, who constituted a large pool of labor under-utilized by the marketplace.

On entering this last quarter of the century, women's employment problems lie not in an inability to find jobs but in an inability to find jobs commensurate with their abilities and rising expectations. For many reasons—stereotyping in education,
training, and hiring practices; intermittency; immobility; the demands of a dual career; discrimination—there appears to be a
wide discrepancy between the career aspirations of women, particularly young women, and the realities of the labor market. It
may well be that this discrepancy is equally applicable to young
men; that what is being revealed is an overall imbalance between
the supply of educated youth and the demand for labor now being generated in the economy. But the position of women is particularly vulnerable in a tight labor market in any event, for they
face the further barriers imposed by the stereotype that grew out
of another era and the continuing demands of dual careers. Attitudes based on assumptions of male-market/female-domestic
work patterns clearly conflict with current trends and expectations for both young men and women.

Declining birth rates, along with rising levels of education and
career aspirations of younger women, suggest that the future
worklives of the two sexes will come to be more nearly the same.
But since the dual career pattern for women seems likely to continue, a series of policy questions is posed. Can part-time and
other flexible work arrangements be made for men and women
in order to permit a more even distribution of both market and
non-market work? Will education and training programs be re-
vamped to offer a wider range of occupational choice to youth of
both sexes? What kinds of child care plans will meet the needs of
a society in which both parents are at work, or only one parent, a
working one, is present? What will be the effect on the provision
of numerous voluntary welfare services of the movement of
larger proportions of women into market work?

The restructuring necessary to accommodate the changing sex
composition of the workforce is pervasive, extending to questions
of working time and scheduling, education and training programs, arrangements for the provision of services formerly provided in the home. One central set of considerations has to do
with the value of home work and free time, and with the allocation of market and nonmarket work between men and women.
For when the division of work and free time is no longer made
on the basis of sex, the lines of responsibility become even more

blurred and appraising the worth of home services and free time, as compared with market goods, becomes even more complex. Yet the allocation of family resources, including that important dimension, time, will have a major effect on the quality of family life.

Harris T. Schrank and John W. Riley, Jr.

4

Women in Work Organizations

Introduction

A large proportion of all employed women is to be found in formally organized work settings: in simple and complex bureaucracies, under local and cosmopolitan managements, in organizations producing both services and goods, in work environments where women have traditionally been employed and where they are relative newcomers.

Statistics are not readily available to indicate precisely how many employed women are in such work organizations, but the evidence suggests that it is a large and growing majority. Over the past two decades, for example, the proportion of women workers engaged in clerical and service occupations, largely based in organizations, has increased sharply, whereas compensating declines are to be noted among individual operatives and private household workers. For males, the situation is quite dif-

HARRIS T. SCHRANK *is Director, Office of Social Research, The Equitable Life Assurance Society of the U.S. Dr. Schrank has taught sociology at Rutgers University and Hunter College. He is on the Board of Directors of the National Council on the Aging. Prior to his formal retirement* JOHN W. RILEY, JR. *was the Senior Vice President for Social Research at The Equitable Life Assurance Society of the U.S. Currently he serves as a consultant both to The Equitable and the Institute of Life Insurance. Dr. Riley has served as Chairman of the Department of Sociology at Rutgers and has been a member of the faculty of four other colleges. He is a trustee of a number of organizations, including the American Foundation for the Blind and the National Urban League. Dr. Riley has been the co-author of four books and was editor of* The Corporation and Its Public.

ferent. Self-employment at most occupational levels, notably as independent professionals, managers or proprietors, continues to thrive as a male tradition in the American economy.

The dramatic increase in total labor force participation of women is well known. There is some difference of view as to how this increase is to be explained, what groups of women are most involved, and what the future holds. The theme of this chapter is that aggregate data on labor force participation cannot tell the full story of what has been happening to women in the workplace. The data must be disaggregated, at least on a case study basis. What *kinds* of work are they doing? How do they move through work organizations? Has sex-stereotyping been curbed? When we look at individual organizations and the structure of jobs within them, do we find that the "revolution" in the labor force participation of women has changed anything in these structures? Can we gauge the probable future of women holding jobs in work organizations? It is to questions such as these that we address ourselves.

Our objective is necessarily modest and our focus of attention narrow. We seek only to cast light on the work status of women at the micro level. We assume that since most women are employed in work organizations of various kinds, knowledge as to the patterns of their employment in these organizations will help to foretell future job opportunities.

The first section of this chapter describes the status of women in a single complex organization. It is intended to supplement the common understanding of the changing work status of women, as shown in aggregate data on labor force participation. The organization under study is not assumed to be "typical" or "representative." Obviously, given the variety of modern work settings, no single organization can be so regarded—but since all organizations have some characteristics in common, we can focus on certain commonalities. The picture of the distribution of jobs that emerges from this case study is apparently one of gross sex inequality. To help explain (although not explain away) this gender-differentiated pattern, the concept of sex-linked job pools, in contrast to pools of jobs unrelated to sex, is introduced. We make a sharp analytical distinction between jobs and people.

The second section develops the concept of job pool in more theoretical terms. We stress the fact that the disparate aggregate patterns of labor force participation (reported elsewhere in this volume) are not based simply upon social factors related to sex, such as differences in education or number of years worked. Instead, we argue that the sex-typing of jobs is so pervasive that only recently have its dimensions been understood in any profound sense. Depending upon one's perspective, the sex-stereotyping of jobs can be either a boring truism—at once obvious, ingrained, conventional, and for some, even perhaps appropriate—or it can be an astonishing revelation of discrimination, polarization of the sexes, subversion, exploitation. There is, in fact, a wide disparity in attitudes toward sex-stereotyping in the work context (regardless of the sex of those holding such views). Where there was once a virtual consensus about appropriate roles, there is now dissension which foretells a process of changing social definitions. The stereotypes of sex roles are suddenly more visible and less acceptable. However, views and attitudes may be changing at different rates than the actual structure and allocation of jobs. In exploring the gender of jobs, our theoretical focus is on pools of jobs rather than on pools of labor to fill the jobs. Our practical focus is at the micro-level of social organization—a focus designed to clarify the manner in which change occurs, the barriers that prevent faster change, and the prospects for greater equality of opportunity in work organizations.

In order to set these rather theoretical remarks on the sex-linked nature of job pools in the context of empirical reality, we conclude our chapter with a brief reexamination of the work status of women in the organization under examination as of five years ago. Using 1970 as a benchmark, it is evident that a process of change has been set in motion even during this brief period. The main thrust of the analysis is to call attention to the glacial inertia created by sex-linked job pools. From this perspective, the long-term occupational future for women in work organizations such as the one under study appears bright.

The Organization under Study

The organization is a large bureaucracy of some 14,000 nonsales employees, composed of managerial/professional, administrative, and clerical workers. There is a home office operation, and it is here that most of the managerial and professional employees work, with about half of the jobs in the home office classifiable as clerical. The field operation consists largely of clerical workers, a smattering of managerial people, and practically no professionals. The home office organization is probably a rough prototype, in structure, composition, and in large part function, of many service bureaucracies, *e.g.*, banks, insurance companies, large advertising and accounting firms, headquarter components of industrial and manufacturing firms, government agencies. Several of the traditional professions are represented in the home office (*e.g.*, law and medicine), together with such "newer" professions as computer specialists, operations research and investment analysts, actuaries, and psychologists. As is common in bureaucracies of this type, some jobs involve both managerial and professional training.

About two-thirds of all employees are women: three-quarters of the field employees, over half of home office employees. In general, women at the company are younger than men. Most women are under thirty, and there are far more women than men of this age in both the field and home office. Among field employees, there are more women than men at all age categories. In the home office, there are more men than women over thirty. The distribution of women among age groups in the field is comparable to the pattern in the home office in several ways: large numbers in the twenty to twenty-nine bracket, much smaller numbers in the thirty to forty-four brackets, a slight increase among those aged forty-five to forty-nine. There are noticeably smaller numbers in the post-thirty age strata among women, but these variations should not be interpreted as representing a "career pattern" for women. These data represent only a cross section or snapshot of the current employee force, and can therefore tell us little about how long people stay at the company, or what the typical career lines are like.

Almost twice as many women as men (1,019 women, 547 men) in the home office have less than two years of service at the company, in strong contrast to the over six times as many women as men in the field with less than two years service (1,796 women, 269 men). Correlatively, about a third more of the men than of the women have more than ten years of experience. Still, this amounts to a sizeable number of women with ten years or more of service—1,700 in the home office and field combined. Two-thirds of the women did not go beyond high school (12 percent with less than four years of high school, 56 percent high school only), while only one-third of the men fall into this category. Forty-five percent of all the men, compared to 13 percent of the women, have a bachelor's degree or have pursued post graduate work. Plainly, there are marked educational differences between men and women in the organization.

In sum, the women are younger than the men, have worked fewer years with the company, and have fewer years of formal education.

KINDS OF WORK: WHO DOES WHAT

Table 1 summarizes the sex structure of jobs by types of work. The job categories are, of course, exceedingly gross, including many different types of jobs. The clerical category, for example, includes file clerks, messengers, and a variety of jobs involving the handling and processing of papers and forms. Most of these jobs are held by people who have not gone beyond high school. The administrative jobs are typically high level clerical jobs which are also thought of as subprofessional jobs, involving the analysis of forms, management of clerical activities, etc. It is in these jobs that college graduates begin to appear; they are, in fact, common entry-level positions for college graduates. Secretarial jobs, somewhat more precisely defined than either administrative or clerical positions, involve typing, stenography, and filing. Practically all such jobs are held by women, in both the field and home office. Professional and managerial jobs are the highest level positions, including professionals and middle and top level managers. There is wide range of job activities, levels of responsibility and pay in this category of jobs.

The secretarial jobs clearly comprise a "female job pool" in both sectors of the organization. (By "female job pool" we mean a set of jobs, in an organization, socially defined as appropriately held only by women. Later we will further delineate the characteristics of such job pools.) The overwhelming proportion of women in this pool is striking and gives the impression of a "caste" differentiation of job pools. It should be emphasized that these figures provide a statistical image of employees in an organization which is the current outcome of historical factors, such as the nature of the labor supply, and above all, the hiring and training system in operation before the organization undertook affirmative action to redress imbalances.

The clerical category represents an interesting variation. In the

TABLE 1. DISTRIBUTION OF TYPES OF WORK BY SEX

	Clerical		Home Office Secretarial		Administrative		Professional/ Managerial	
	N	%	N	%	N	%	N	%
Male	635	30.2	12	1.2	1,009	50.5	1,210	79.6
Female	1,470	69.8	983	98.8	988	49.5	310	20.4
				Field				
Male	116	7.1	22	1.0	390	42.4	868	70.2
Female	1,529	92.9	2,250	99.0	530	57.6	369	29.8

field, it will be remembered, the vast preponderance of those holding such positions are women, and this suggests that the clerical category of jobs is just another case of a sex-linked pool. But in the home office, fully 30 percent of the clerical workers are men. Clearly this pool of jobs is not nearly as sex-linked as it is in the field.

There are several probable reasons for this difference in the sex linkage of clerical pools in the home office and field. First, there is a *general* tendency for lower-level jobs in the clerical pool to be held disproportionately by women and there are proportionately more lower-level clerical jobs in the field. Secondly, there is a greater variety of clerical jobs in the home office than in the field and some subcategories of clerks have substantial proportions of males. There is a third possibility: that the home office has a different type of hiring system than the field; that the sex criteria for employment operate differently in the two contexts. Though we have scant data on the subject we know that in the field hiring is done locally, in about two hundred different locations; possibly local norms operate to place women in these jobs. In the home office there is a tradition of having men as well as women in the low level clerical positions. As we will note below, a few of these positions have historically been defined as starting points for upward mobility. Currently, for example, there are several dozen very high level executives—all males—who began their careers in such jobs.

The two other job categories are mixed. The professional/ managerial pool is largely male in both contexts; the administrative pool is defined as mostly female in the field, male in the home office. In each context, for each pool, the higher level jobs are predominantly held by males, lower level jobs by females. Indeed, for these jobs, there is more sex variation by levels than by pools. At the highest levels, irrespective of pools, the vast proportion of jobs is held by males. But it is instructive to note that job levels within these job pools are sex linked in various degrees. In contrast, the predominantly female job pools (*i.e.*, secretarial in the home office and field, clerical in the field) are sex-segregated, regardless of job level.

The paradigm for sex-linked job pools further indicates that job pools have different levels, and that female jobs have lower levels than male jobs. There is a clear aggregate relationship here, *i.e.*, the secretarial pool is a relatively low-level pool. In the field it is the lowest level pool whereas in the home office it is the second lowest, next to clerk. In each location, administrative is the second highest level, and professional and managerial the highest. Such aggregate data strongly support the notion that female job pools contain relatively low level positions. To examine this issue in somewhat greater detail we need to look at the problem of job level directly.

As noted, females on the average hold lower level jobs than males. This is not surprising, insofar as women at the company are generally much younger, have fewer years of service, and have completed less formal education than males. When these gross descriptive variables are held constant, sex differences in job levels tend to lessen, but some differences remain. For example, slightly over half of the home office women whose education did not go beyond high school are in jobs in the bottom quarter of the job hierarchy, while less than 30 percent of the men in this education category have jobs at this level. At the other extreme of the hierarchy, only about 3 percent of the women with less than a high school education are in positions in the top half of the continuum, compared with nearly one-third of the men in this educational category. There are differences by sex—not quite so extreme—among other educational strata. When length of service is taken into account, some differences also remain—women continue to have lower level positions.

Notes on the Concept of Job Pools

In presenting a statistical profile of the organization under study, we found it analytically convenient to distinguish between people and jobs. Hence the notion that a pool of jobs can be differentiated from the everyday idea of a labor pool (or pool of workers) seems to warrant further exploration. Indeed, it is our hypothesis that the concept of job pools may turn out to have significant power to explain the problems of women in a changing economy. The data show certain jobs, or "families" of jobs, are defined as appropriately male, female, or without gender. Recall that we are speaking here of jobs, or positions, not of the people who hold the jobs or occupy the positions. As such, job pools have quite distinct and observable characteristics.

Having examined these job pools in one organizational context, and on the basis of some pertinent literature on the nature of jobs within organizations, we propose next to explore variations among pools with respect to two considerations: hierarchical and differential patterns of upward mobility, and dependency status. Our approach to this subject is exploratory and tentative, since the notion of the sex-linked job pool, as we use it, is neither well-specified nor widely used within social science literature. First, let us discuss the meaning of hierarchy and upward mobility within each of the two sex-linked pools. In our concluding note we shall pay particular attention to the neuter or "gender-free" pool.

HIERARCHY AND MOBILITY

All jobs within large organizations appear to have some position within a hierarchy. That is, they tend to be pegged at certain salary and status levels. Some jobs, however, are part of a general organizational hierarchy; other jobs are hierarchical only within specified limits. There is, for example, a hierarchy of secretarial jobs, but it has an upper limit well below the highest level of jobs within the organization. Many clerk jobs are similarly positioned. The level of a job is not an accurate indicator of how it is positioned within a hierarchy. For example, entry level or first level jobs have traditionally been part of a hierarchy leading up a ladder or web to higher level positions. It is our observation that such jobs have been traditionally, although perhaps not currently, held by males, and have been defined as male jobs.

Female entry level positions, with comparable pay and perhaps comparable prestige (*e.g.*, secretary, file clerk), have not functioned in this manner. An occupant in the female pool of jobs

has for the most part been precluded from the same sort of hierarchical movement that is found in the male pool of jobs. Of
course, there has been some potential for upward mobility within
the female pool, but change, if it occurred, was slower and more
limited in range. The upper limit for the male pool is the president's position. The comparable upper limit job within the female pool is often secretary to the president. Hence, as shown in
Figure 1, the upper level female job is located at a rank comparable to, say, the middle level male position.

Fig. 1. Ranking in Sex-linked Job Pools

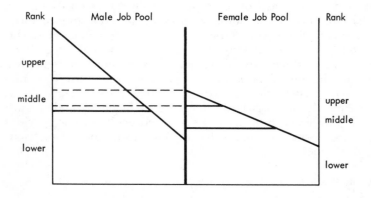

We are not certain what proportion of jobs would be regarded
as upper or lower rank within each of the pools. We do hypothesize, however, that different ranks can be attributed to jobs
within each of the pools. We further hypothesize that with respect to a general social standard, the ranks between pools are
not equivalent. A job seen as upper rank within the female pool
is not perceived as upper rank considering all jobs, or considering jobs within the male pool. At this stage we cannot say very
much about the magnitude of the difference in mobility potential
between the two pools except that it is probably quite sizeable.

DEPENDENCY STATUS

Dependency status, our second consideration in exploring the
nature of jobs in the male and female pools, is high for women
in industrial organizations because the ranking of jobs in the fe-

male pool is likely, to borrow Veblen's term, to be "vicarious"—that is, to be dependent upon the ranks of the associated male pool jobs. For example, the secretary at the highest rank in the female pool gains prestige in a manner quite different from the way prestige is gained in the male pool. The latter is gained through managerial control, staff authority (in the sense of expertise), control over assets, or salary. The secretary, by contrast, gains prestige by being related to a prestigious male job. Her prestige is vicarious.

Vicarious rank holds for many other jobs, especially staff positions that have "assistant to" (written explicitly or implicitly) into their descriptions. Let us call this status relationship—between jobs within male and female job pools—dependency status, simply because the status of the female job is dependent upon the male job. The converse is *not* the case. The rank of a male job is never dependent upon the rank of a female job. This is because the rank of the male job is higher than that of the female job to which it is related. There are jobs in the female pool that have higher status than jobs within the male pool, but these female jobs are not systematically related to male jobs of lower rank. A high ranking secretary job (female pool) may have other lower-ranking jobs related to it (*e.g.*, assistant secretary or file clerk) but the lower level jobs are in the female pool. Such female jobs continue to have vicarious rank—rank derived from the female job superior to it, but ultimately from the male job which forms the primary source of rank for that employment unit.

A comparable phenomenon of vicarious rank is well-known in the family. Only recently, for example, have sociologists begun to measure a wife's social rank by looking at anything other than her husband's occupation.

Within the business organization, to be sure, male and female jobs are often complementary. But they are always hierarchical, with the rank of the male job superior. Patterns of exchange typically develop, and both partners to this dyad actually enjoy or perceive the reality of mutual gains. We are not privy to any research on this subject and hence can only speculate on the nature of such dyads. It seems plausible that a vast variety of relationships exist among pairs, where the two parties have reached some way of dividing functions, rewards, authority, so they can work together. The formal classification of jobs, with various degrees of compensation and assigned authority tells us little about who does what. Indeed, one suspects that the holder of the female job *actually* does many of the things which the male job holder is supposed to do.

Such patterns of job hierarchy and dependency indicate that people are not allocated to jobs irrespective of their gender. Instead, there are well established and structured patterns of job allocation by sex, reflecting socialization patterns, cultural beliefs, and perceptions in the larger society. In the next section we suggest that a well-known model of stratification—the caste system—helps us to understand this structure.

THE CASTE ANALOGY

The classic statement on caste by the anthropologist A. L. Kroeber defines it as "an endogenous and hereditary subdivision of an ethnic unit occupying a position of superior or inferior rank or social esteem in comparison with other such subdivisions." Our use of the term caste is an adaptation by analogy in several respects. First, we are not dealing with "an ethnic unit." Second, we apply it only to a structure of specific roles (*i.e.*, jobs) rather than to a generalized system of ranking. Third, we do not deal with hereditary claims, except by an expanded notion of what that term ordinarily means. Nevertheless, we have identified a relatively rigid system of social stratification, and the notion of superior versus inferior rank is appropriate to the term caste.

The concept of caste is useful in explaining the relative lack of movement from one pool to another, or "crossing over." Quite obviously, if there is indeed a caste situation, there will be no movement of people from one caste to another, and this is what is typically found; there is virtually *no* movement of people from the male job pool to the female job pool. Here we need again to emphasize that we distinguish jobs from people. While movement from the male to the female job pool is virtually unheard of, there is, however, some mobility from the female pool to the male pool.

Women are socialized to assume roles within the female pool and subsequently are allocated roles within that pool. They have by social definition been relegated to positions inferior in rank to those allocated to the male pool. Conversely, those socialized and allocated into the male pool have not been labelled, relatively speaking; they have been trained to value all manner of requisites and opportunities unavailable in the female pool. For them to move into the female pool jobs would be unthinkable. It would, quite literally under present circumstances, be the equivalent to a fall from grace. This explains why male "crossing" is so rare. In terms of social rewards, to be unemployed is the more appealing alternative. Correlatively, there is a stigma attached to holding a position in the lower rank (female) pool, even for a woman. A woman "chosen" to move out of that pool may bear the burden of her formerly low, dependent status—she will have more to overcome than if her previous rank were unknown.

For an incumbent of a female pool job to move out of that pool and cross over to the male pool is not rare. This move is perceived by both male and female incumbents as a positive development, conferring added rank, prestige, and often money. This seems quite appealing on its face; who, given the opportunity, would hesitate to leave a lower caste for a higher one? Yet there are many cases where a female role incumbent prefers not to cross over to assume the new role. While we cannot explain this preference in all or even most cases, it seems likely that a woman whose significant reference group consists of others in the female pool, would find it difficult to move outside that context. What is crucial is the recognition of uneven parallel ranks across pools. Women in female jobs can, in a very real sense, lose rank by crossing over to male jobs.

This problem is further intensified when a woman worker from the female pool holds a job related to a high ranking male position. We have discussed the dependent or vicarious prestige of female jobs related to a high ranking male job. We have also noted that it is common for the woman who holds such a job to create a mutually beneficial dyadic relationship with the holder of the "dominant" (male) job. There is, in short, substantial sex segregation built into the structure of jobs based on the differing ranks of jobs in each pool.

This segregation persists, despite the fact that opportunities for learning valuable organizational skills needed for upward mobility are provided by jobs from the female pool. For example, many female jobs "tied" to higher ranked male jobs would probably provide superb training experience for upward mobility. It is a commonplace observation that many women, especially secretaries, actually perform many of the tasks that constitute the associated male job. Such women are brought into decision-making and they exercise control over the male incumbent's subordinates. If one were to construct a training job that would allow the trainee to see and participate in the work of a higher ranking office, the design in many respects might resemble the secretarial job. Yet organizations commonly fail to capitalize on this experience by moving female job pool incumbents into higher ranking male gender-free pool jobs. This is surprising in view of the generally held notion—going back to the tradition of thought associated with Max Weber—that bureaucracies are highly rational-efficient structures.

What accounts for this organizational inefficiency? Why are female pool jobs not generally training jobs for higher ranking positions in other job pools?

Socialization patterns in childhood offer some clues. There appears to be a continuity between early female roles and workplace roles. While the objective tasks of the female job could be perceived as providing experience for many jobs outside the female job pool, the job is not ordinarily so perceived. It is, rather, commonly perceived as a circumscribed "helping" role; initiative is not highly rewarded except within strictly prescribed limits. Performance is assessed in terms of effectiveness in assisting a higher ranking job incumbent rather than in demonstrating skills suggesting a capacity to assume a higher ranking job. Upward mobility is frequently attained through attachment to an upwardly mobile male job pool incumbent. Aggressiveness is negatively sanctioned. Management of others is constrained; only where it is in a representative capacity (representing the associated higher ranked job) is it tolerated.

Within the organization, but outside job performance situations, the female reference group is comprised not of men, or incumbents of male jobs, but of women. Observation of seating patterns in the cafeteria of a large corporation will demonstrate the striking sex segregation; whether self-imposed or not we do not know. Women cannot trade information crucial to performance of male jobs if their contact with males is thus constrained. As in any caste system, social isolation is operative. Hence, another reason that the female job is not, in fact, a step toward a male job.

The organization may appear in many ways to gain through maintaining this perception of female jobs. For example, economically the "costs" of jobs seem to be lower. But, we can only speculate at the economic and social costs to an organization arising from sex segregation. For example, as suggested above, costs are likely to be higher because of an organization's inability to promote women into higher ranking positions and thus utilize fully the experience of female job incumbents. At the same time the sex-linked system appears to conform with perceived wishes of female job holders. That is, the female pool may be perceived and defined by those allocating jobs as well as by those applying for them as providing some respite from the costs of being located in the hierarchical and competitive male job pool. Yet there is, in fact, little or no reason to believe that the female pool is less competitive than the male pool. And the female pool *is* hierarchical. The organizational gains flowing from ordinary assumptions maintaining the sex-linked system may, then, be illusory.

How much of the real world does such a job pool analysis explain? While we stress that the concept of job pool is still undeveloped, we suggest only that it does help to understand our earlier presentation of data. It also calls attention to potential variations among work organizations regarding patterns of jobholding by sex. Some organizations are run and staffed entirely by members of a single sex. Others have few jobs that are sex-linked and still others have jobs that show relatively little congruence between the sex-definition of jobs and the actual sex of the incumbent. But among most work organizations on which we have systematic data there is an extremely high congruence on this point. In the real world of today, many jobs continue to be sex-linked.

Why, then, is sex in fact an important criterion for job allocation? First, we suggest that the distribution rests on the entrenched perception held by people who operate the allocative process that sex is a relevant performance criterion. That is, people who hire people, or who are related in any way to the hiring process, treat sex as a characteristic related to the ability of a potential job incumbent. This perception accounts in large part for the sex-linked nature of the *demand* for people to fill jobs.

But we need also to note the nature of the supply—the characteristics, and size of the pool of *people* available to fill existing or potential jobs. The notion of supply, applied to women workers, is admittedly imprecise because of its traditionally fluctuating nature. This is largely because more women than men exercise choice as to whether and when they enter the labor force. Furthermore, a relatively high proportion have part-time jobs, and many move in and out of the labor force as they have children, or relocate their families.

On the other hand, characterization of the supply side in terms of training, education, and experience is in one sense a more precise and estimable matter. In some cases, there simply are very few women trained or experienced in certain professions (*e.g.*, accounting, engineering, architecture). Similarly, there may be few men available to fill certain female roles. And, of course, in other cases there are simply few people of either sex available to fill needed roles. But there may be a plethora of people of one sex available to fill certain roles (*e.g.*, secretary). In these cases an organization, recruiting people at relatively late stages in the life course, tends to recruit and process people as they are available, accepting the social and demographic givens. To do otherwise is to incur additional costs. For example, if schools and training institutions fail to train males for secretarial jobs, an organization desiring male secretaries would have to train them, thus absorbing costs which would not be involved if it were simply to assume recruitment and allocative patterns consistent with the available supply. It would be inordinately naive to assume, however, that the supply side is not strongly affected by the perceived needs of work organizations. Organizations obviously make known, overtly or covertly, what is needed, and consequently contribute to traditional societal patterns. Advertising, representation of products, corporate gifts, selling and distributing patterns, as well as hiring practices, all contain signals to those involved in developing the supply of workers. And the characteristics of the supply reflect these implicit messages of work organizations.

Still, work organizations can sometimes shift priorities quickly. A change in the economic environment of an organization may suddenly produce a need for more people to fill certain roles, thereby opening up opportunities for members of one sex where the other has had a monopoly on a particular pool of jobs. Or legal and political considerations can require a reappraisal of the sex pattern of demand. In such instances, the criteria for filling jobs will broaden; special training programs in organizations will develop, and organizations will more actively change the criteria for allocating people to jobs.

More specific knowledge of the internal dynamics of work organizations is obviously required if the articulation of supply and demand resulting in varying patterns of job holding by sex is to be understood, and the allocative mechanism is to be adjusted to bring about greater equality of opportunity for women. Below, we offer a basic approach to the analysis of this problem in organizations.

COHORT FLOW THROUGH JOB POOLS

One effective method of studying change in work organizations is to examine a cohort—an aggregate of new recruits hired within a specific period of time—and to note the patterns of mobility for various subsets of this group. This method of cohort analysis helps us to learn *how* the cross-sectional picture was formed.

For the case study sketched above, we examined the cohort of recruits entering the organization in 1971, and traced their mobility patterns over a four-year period. For those who entered at the lowest ranks—and there were quite large numbers of recruits who assumed these entry-level positions—quite different patterns of mobility emerged for males and females. Almost all the males either received promotions or left the organization within a year or two after being hired. Of the males who did receive promotions, a high proportion stayed. But among females, a substantial proportion of those who received no promotion within the first year or two stayed. And surprisingly, among those women who received several promotions, a higher proportion than among the "successful" males left the organization. Thus, after four years, the original cohort was relatively over-represented by nonmobile females and highly mobile males, even though mobility rates were comparable for members of both sexes. The unsophisticated observer, looking at the patterns of mobility for men and women who had stayed in the organization, might conclude that women had experienced lower mobility than men. But this conclusion would be quite incorrect—mobile women and nonmobile men had simply left.

At higher entry level jobs these patterns did not hold; indeed, it was often difficult to establish different mobility patterns for males and females. It is interesting to note that retention rates among females are not consistently different than for males; within some categories they are higher, others lower. Among college graduates who entered a special organizational trainee program, for example, retention was higher for women than men. Many observers might find this to be a counter-intuitive outcome.

These comments illustrate the desirability of in-depth cohort analysis of job mobility patterns in work organizations. Such analysis can expose fallacious assumptions about which persons are committed to upwardly mobile careers, whether in organizations males follow different paths of mobility than females, and whether patterns of discrimination are evident. It is to the last question that we address our concluding remarks.

Concluding Note: Discrimination and Job Pools

In our society "achievement" or performance criteria have traditionally been regarded as paramount in formulating personnel policies. These are criteria which directly represent past attainments. Such criteria are thought to be relevant to the actual job requirements and to indicate future performance. Sociologists and other observers have noted that achievement criteria are typically associated or correlated with ascriptive characteristics, such as age, race, or sex. We need not discuss here the reasons for this correlation between performance potential and ascriptive characteristics, save to note that they obviously include prior discrimination and socialization practices. We note merely that by invoking an apparently legitimate criterion, *i.e.,* achievement, in the allocation process, job allocating agents have effectively removed women from consideration for many jobs.

When allocators apply probabilities of performance to categories of people, and allocate in terms of these probabilities, regardless of the capabilities of individuals within the category, a kind of discrimination results which we call "probability discrimination." This type of discrimination is based upon a known, or perceived statistical relationship between an ascriptive characteristic and the potential job performance of people having this characteristic. For example, if it is generally perceived within an organization that women are ineffective managers on the basis, say, of a few cases, organization policies or practices may develop which inhibit the assignment of women to managerial jobs. A pattern of discrimination thus emerges based on a statistical relationship (which, in itself may clearly reflect fallacious assumptions of prior personnel practices). Often, as in our example, the empirical basis for probability discrimination is weak. It has become observable that allocation agents have not always adhered strictly to achievement criteria, but have used ascriptive criteria directly without any empirical basis, thereby excluding some capable people, and categories of people, from certain jobs (and choosing others). Where the ascriptive criteria so invoked are clearly irrelevant to estimates of job performance, we can apply the term "invidious discrimination" to the process. Unlike probability discrimination, invidious discrimination is essentially arbitrary, and rests on no empirical base—actual or assumed.

The recent movement from the use of achievement criteria to ascriptive criteria is largely attributable to probability and invidious discrimination operative within the system, and to subsequent efforts to correct the system itself. Indeed, ascriptive criteria, notably sex, age, and race, are now explicitly used in order to assure enlarged opportunities for different categories of people.

We suggest that though the use of sex as a criterion for discrimination has been manifested by both invidious and probability discrimination, the latter type of discrimination has been most common. This is to say that discrimination applied to women has often been based upon perceived variations in the probability that they would perform as adequately on a job, or as long on the job, as men. Recent survey data consistently show that a majority of men support the women's movement and equal opportunity for women, and that this support often exceeds the support women themselves give to such issues. Such data are consistent with the hypothesis that sex discrimination in organizations is not invidious, not intractable. Further, that the discrimination implicit in sex-linked job pools is inexorably changing has been the central thrust both of the empirical description of one organization and our theoretical discussion of the problem.

Over the past few years, the organization under study gives clear indication of changes in woman's "place." During this period several intervening factors have been operative:

1. The mix of traditional and non-traditional jobs has been altered in large measure due to professionalization and computerization. Thus many more new types of jobs have been created and these have evolved into gender-free pools. For example, historical data on the composition of job pools indicate that only five years ago the professional/managerial pool in the field was over 90 percent male, placing it well within our caste model as a sex-linked pool. Today, this job pool, with 70 percent males, is taking on characteristics of a gender-free pool. Over five times as many women now have field jobs within that pool, 70 in 1970 and 369 in 1975.

2. In both the home office and field offices, strong affirmative action programs have been pursued and goals have been set to give new emphasis to the ascriptive criterion of sex—thus providing wider opportunities for women at all job levels.

3. A new company policy was promulgated which opened up the traditionally male-dominated sales force. Thus, an entirely new career
for women—a new job pool—was developed. In 1970 there were
under one hundred women in the sales force; today there are over
three hundred. The future development of this new career will be
a fascinating story, since it is a break within a traditional male bas-
tion; however it would be premature at this time to speculate on
the probable success of this new policy.

While the necessary data are not available to enable us to
weigh the relative impact of these three changes, there are mea-
surable differences in the extent to which women occupy the
more desirable positions in the organization. The data show the
organization to be in the midst of a rapid transition in the movement of women to higher ranked positions, and that these positions tend *not* to be found in sex-linked job pools. In 1970 there
were 154 women with jobs in the top half of the job hierarchy; in
1975 there were exactly three times as many women holding
such jobs (462). In comparison, there was a modest 24 percent
increase in the number of men holding such positions, although
the actual number of male occupied positions was over five times
as large as those held by women. This change has not occurred
merely because of an influx of new college trained women. Mobility has been dramatic among women with many years of service or modest educational backgrounds. For example, among
the home office women with no formal education beyond high
school, the number of women in the middle management level
(or higher) increased from eleven in 1970 to eighty-three in
1975.

The list of such changes could be extended but the point
would be lost for, in each instance, the numerical gains have
been slight. Yet the point not to be lost is that gains have been
made. And this suggests that subtle changes have taken place in
the nature of job pools; gender-free pools have become increasingly significant.

Gender-free pools are more likely to be found in fast growing
or new sectors of organizations, where there has been a lively demand for people to fill jobs, and hence, where invocation of the
sex criterion would inhibit recruitment. In many large service organizations, including our case for example, the computer-
oriented professions—*e.g.*, programming, operations research—

have represented gender-free areas of employment. In these areas traditional norms often simply do not exist. Similarly, there are fewer constraints on socialization into such jobs, it may still be "socially inappropriate" for women to become engineers or accountants, but no such comparable tradition, to our knowledge, has developed, for example, regarding computer specialists or systems analysts. Perhaps such fields have grown so fast they never had time to establish a sexual identity. One implication of this observation is that as new jobs or job families develop, they will tend to be gender-free pools. This bodes well for the future employment of women.

The glacial ice in the sex-linked job pools is beginning to thaw. It seems clear that affirmative action programs which pay proper heed to the ascriptive criterion of sex are contributing significantly to the thaw. Yet perhaps of equal or even greater importance are the policy decisions and social and economic forces which are creating gender-free job pools. The time may not be far off when the traditional criterion of achievement, irrespective of sex, may be fairly and appropriately employed in the allocation of people to jobs.

Kristin A. Moore and Isabel V. Sawhill

5

Implications of Women's Employment for Home and Family Life

Introduction

Over the last few decades, an unprecedented rise in the employment rate of married women has significantly altered the economic role of women while the emergence of a new feminist movement in the early 1960s has influenced many people's perceptions of women's "place" in our society. Given women's traditional commitment to home and children—a commitment which now appears to be weakening as new options become available—it would be surprising if these changes in the status of women were to have no impact on the American family. And in fact there is evidence of widespread dislocation in that venerable institution. Demographers have faithfully recorded some of the essential changes. They have found a rise in the age at which young women marry, a dramatic upsurge in divorce rates, and a sharp decline in birth rates together with a rise in the proportion of births occurring outside of marriage. While these changes can-

ISABEL V. SAWHILL *is a Senior Research Associate and Director of a Program of Research on Women at The Urban Institute. She was Chairperson of the Department of Economics at Goucher College. Dr. Sawhill has written numerous articles and papers, and was the co-author of the book* Time of Transition: The Growth of Families Headed by Women. KRISTIN ANDERSON MOORE *is a Research Associate at The Urban Institute. Previously, Dr. Moore was a sociology instructor at the University of Michigan and a teaching fellow with the Detroit Area Study.*

not be definitively linked to changes in the social or economic position of women, there is some evidence that these two sets of trends are not unrelated, and it is quite possible that the shifts in family structure which have occurred to date are only minor harbingers of much more fundamental shifts to come.

The increased employment of women means that they will have less time to devote to home and family and more economic resources that enable them to choose a wider variety of possibly less family-oriented lifestyles. These possibilities, in turn, raise questions about the welfare of children, the size of families, the stability of marriages, the quality of relationships between men and women, the division of labor within the household, and the distribution of family income. What changes have already occurred in each of these areas, if any, and what kinds of new policy issues are raised by the prospect of further change? Can society adjust to, even plan for, these changes? Or will we merely muddle through?

The Future of Marriage

THE ECONOMIC AND SOCIAL BASIS OF MARRIAGE

In the past women have had few opportunities to earn a living on an equal basis with men; as a result, marriage has been essential to women's economic welfare. Economists—who view the married household as a small unit of production which allocates the time of its various members among different tasks according to each individual's talents—argue that as long as women are at least as efficient as men in producing household goods and services but have lower market earnings, the most efficient allocation of resources requires that women specialize in home production and men in market production. Through marriage each can gain the benefits from this specialization. Thus, the traditional division of labor between husbands and wives is in part economically determined, although social expectations clearly play a major role as well. The consequence of this particular division of labor is that wives are dependent on their husbands for those necessities of life which can be bought only in the market. Although much has been made of the implicit value of a housewife's services, the important fact is that in our market-oriented society these homemaking services command a high return in the form of other goods, services, and prestige only *within the context of the family*.

Even in our present, partially-liberated culture, the most important decision a young woman faces is likely to be the choice of whom to marry. Unlike her male counterpart, she must bear in mind that her social and economic standing will depend much more on the outcome of this decision than on her own education, family background, or occupational prospects. To be sure, the latter help to determine whom she associates with and eventually marries, but it is the marriage itself which secures her position within the social system. It is for this reason that a father traditionally worries about a young man's potential ability to support his daughter, that mothers teach their daughters to use female wiles to entice the "right" young man into marriage, and that adolescent girls have often given more thought to marriage than to their own education or career.

In the past, women have had very little choice in these matters. Those who did not marry were viewed with pity, and often had great difficulty earning a living. Few have ever achieved high incomes or status in their own right. Those who have married have happily taken on the usual domestic responsibilities of a wife and mother in response to both social custom and lack of good economic alternatives. This very specialization, of course, leads to still greater dependency, because over the life cycle a wife's productivity within the home increases relative to her productivity in the market while the opposite occurs for men. By the time a woman who has devoted herself to home and family reaches middle-age, she usually has few marketable skills that would enable her to support herself outside of marriage. Thus, she is more dependent than ever on a marital tie. Women's dependence on marriage is further reinforced by a shortage of alternative partners should the first marriage be terminated. The ratio of unmarried women to unmarried men increases dramatically as one moves up through the age range, partly because of higher male mortality rates and partly because men tend to remarry women who are considerably younger than their first wives. As a result, female prospects for remarriage decline precipitously with age.

Marrying and remaining married, then, are economic as well as social necessities for women deprived of an independent means of support. Men, too, tend to be bound to their marriages by a sense of social responsibility to wife and children and by the knowledge that the costs of supporting more than one family may be prohibitively high. One result of this state of affairs is the prevalence of what William Goode has called "empty shell" marriages—marriages in which there is little love or real caring but a reasonably high degree of stability related to social and economic constraints which inhibit formal dissolution of the marriage relationship.

If this is a reasonable description of the traditional marriages which have prevailed, with some modifications, from the beginning of the Industrial Revolution down to the present day, important questions now arise: what will marriages of the future look like, assuming marriage survives? How will they differ from those of the past?

If women move into the labor force in increasing numbers and take a more favored position within the occupational structure, this change will tend to undermine the traditional division of labor within the household and the interdependencies this specialization implies. Marriages based on economic considerations will give way to those in which the utilitarian basis of marriage has been eroded, and love, companionship, and perhaps children remain as the only reasons for maintaining a particular relationship intact. It is likely that these marriages will be less stable than marriages of the past, although those which do endure will probably provide greater satisfaction to the participants than the more economically-motivated and socially-constrained alliances of today.

At the present time, the institution of marriage lies somewhere between the totally egalitarian marriages which could emerge in the future and the highly traditional marriages of the past. Although almost half of married women are working, their jobs are often viewed as secondary to their family responsibilities and their income as supplementary rather than essential. Partly for this reason, but also because of the strength of ingrained attitudes, men have continued to maintain their authority as household heads, to consider their work as primary, and to share little in the unpaid work of the household. Although most American marriages are based on a democratic commitment to shared decision-making, in fact they tend to be partnerships in which the wife is clearly the junior partner and where there are "separate but equal" spheres of influence.

CONSEQUENCES OF WOMEN'S EMPLOYMENT
FOR MARRIAGE AND DIVORCE

The foregoing discussion suggests that the future of marriage is linked to changes in the economic and social status of women. There are already indications that when young unmarried women have high incomes they are less likely to marry (or more likely to postpone marriage), and that when wives work and contribute to family income, a divorce is more likely to occur. A number of studies have now documented the inverse relationship between high education, high earnings, or strong commitment to the labor force among women, on the one hand, and low rates of marriage or high rates of divorce, on the other. Some of the data on this question make it impossible in infer which is cause and which is effect—that is, one possible interpretation is that women who are not very marriageable or who find themselves in a non-married state will be forced to work and will have a greater need to stay in school and earn a good income. Still another possible interpretation is that men may find high-achieving women threatening or less desirable as mates.

Some new research on this question, involving a representative national sample of families whose marital behavior was monitored over a period of years, shows that, other things being equal, the likelihood of divorce is greater where wives have had access to an independent source of income while married. One plausible interpretation of this finding is that, of all the marriages which are tension-ridden or unsatisfactory for some reason, the costs of divorce are lowest for those in which the wives have some capability for self-support. Another possibility is that failure to conform to societal norms about appropriate sex role behavior is itself tension-producing for one or both spouses. Both are probably true. If so, it follows that the recent upsurge in divorce rates reflects both greater economic independence among women and the marital strains engendered by changing attitudes about the position of women.

Once society has adjusted to a new set of more egalitarian norms, the divorce rate might decline somewhat as a result. But if the economic achievements of women continue to undermine the utilitarian character of traditional marriages, a permanently higher rate of divorce is a likely outcome. Furthermore, as divorce becomes more common it will be by definition less deviant and will be viewed as more acceptable; this change in attitudes will further erode the constraints which currently inhibit marital dissolution. Thus, individual marriages may dissolve for countless reasons which have nothing to do with the changing status of women, but it is this more fundamental change in sex roles which creates the environment in which these changing behavior patterns emerge.

At the same time, other forces are at work which may operate to increase rather than reduce the stability of the family. Younger single women now have the economic resources to establish their own independent households before marriage to a much greater extent than in the past. They have less need to marry in order to escape the parental home. For this and other reasons, they are delaying marriage in large numbers and the average age at first marriage has moved up gradually since 1962. If this trend continues or is at least maintained, it will mean greater marital stability in the future since marrying young is highly correlated with later divorce or separation. Thus, as the economic imperatives for women decline, and are accompanied by more permissive attitudes about premarital sex, it is quite possible that young people will choose a mate more slowly and more wisely; the resulting marriages would then rest on a more solid foundation.

RELATIONSHIPS BETWEEN HUSBANDS AND WIVES

A second consequence of women's greater commitment to work and increased access to economic resources is likely to be a shift in the relationships between men and women *within* marriage.

A number of studies have found that wives who are employed exercise a greater degree of power in their marriages. Marital power is higher among women employed full-time rather than part-time or not at all, and it is greatest among women with the most prestigious occupations, women who are most committed to their work, and those whose salaries exceed those of their husbands. In particular, working women have more say in financial decisions. This tendency for employment to enhance women's power within the family is strongest among lower or working class couples.

The resource theory of Robert Blood and Donald Wolfe provides an explanation for these findings:

The sources of power in so intimate a relationship as marriage must be sought in the comparative resources which the husband and wife bring to the marriage, rather than in brute force. A resource may be defined as anything that one partner may make available to the other, helping the latter satisfy his needs or attain his goals. . . . The partner who may provide or withhold resources is in a strategic position. . . . Hence, power accrues spontaneously to the partner who has the greater resources at his disposal.

In accordance with this argument, it is understandable that employed women appear to have more power than nonemployed women: they contribute to family income and their experiences on the job may provide them with valuable new knowledge and contacts. Factors other than income can also act as resources— for example, physical attractiveness, special skills such as cooking or entertaining, a prestigious family background. Working women may lose power, too, if they have to seek help with household tasks that their husbands view as part of a wife's role and for which there are few acceptable substitutes.

The existing literature on marital power has been subjected to some criticism because of the difficulty of measuring and quantifying concepts such as "resources" and "power." But if one accepts the basic theory outlined here, it suggests that as more women move into the labor force and contribute a larger fraction of total family income they will acquire new rights as wives, and improve their bargaining position within marriage. The wife who once had to ask her husband's permission to buy a new dress will be free to make her own decisions about these matters, in addition to having the higher status which generally accrues to income-earning adults.

HOUSEHOLD WORK

Closely related to the issue of marital power is the question of how the employment of women affects both the division of tasks between husband and wife, and the total amount of work carried on within the household. In general, husbands of working wives engage in slightly more child care and housework than do husbands of nonworking women; however, it does not appear that the rapid movement of women into the labor force has been matched by any great increase in husbands' willingness to help around the house.

Data based on household interviews with married couples in Detroit suggest that little change occurred in the distribution of household tasks between 1955 and 1971. Of the tasks considered, three functions are preponderantly the wife's responsibility—doing the dishes, getting breakfast, and straightening up the living room. Decisions about the house, car, life insurance, and the husband's job, as well as responsibility for household repairs, tend to fall into the husband's realm. Grocery shopping, deciding on the food budget, taking care of money and bills and making decisions about the wife's employment are either joint concerns or fall more within the wife's domain. Although some change did occur in the allocation of tasks—for example, husbands were more likely to get their own breakfasts in 1971—the more notable finding was an absence of the kind of change that one might have expected to see accompanying the movement of women from the home into the labor market. Indeed, in 1971, women were *more* likely than in 1955 to do the grocery shopping and the evening dishes and less likely to make decisions about life insurance, about what house or apartment to take, and whether or not they themselves should go to work or quit work.

Clearly, it takes some time for these adjustments to take place. Yet it does not seem, at least for the short run, that women have traded one kind of work for another. They seem instead to have taken on a new set of activities without foregoing their traditional responsibilities. Whether this is because men are still the primary breadwinners in most families (*i.e.*, have substantially higher earnings than their wives), or whether it simply reflects deeply ingrained attitudes that are slow to change is difficult to say.

One sort of accommodation that working women do seem to have made is a reduction in the total number of hours that are spent doing household tasks. Joann Vanek has reported that, despite the existence of new convenience appliances, *nonemployed* urban women spent an average of fifty-five hours per week in the 1960s doing household tasks that *nonemployed* rural women spent fifty-two hours on in 1924. *Employed* women, on the other hand, spent only one-half as many hours on housework. This difference is not due to full-time housewives having more children, younger children, less household help, or a different social class or marital status than employed women. The latter may have lower housekeeping standards, purchase more goods and services in the market (restaurant meals, commercial laundries, etc.), or simply do their work more efficiently. Since working women have thus far gotten little extra household help from their husbands, they have had to compensate for their market work in other ways. For the future, there are likely to be economic and attitudinal changes inducing men to share more fully in the work of the home.

ADJUSTMENTS FOR MEN

Decisions as to who does the housework is only one area in which the increased employment of married women is likely to affect the lives of men. Yet relatively little research has been done on these effects. The traditional role of the male as provider and protector is being challenged as women begin to share and sometimes usurp these roles. Some response on the part of men is inevitable. Mirra Komarovsky, and more recently Matina Horner, have both written on the threat that female competence poses for males. Being married to a woman with a busy schedule, an income of her own, outside friendships and commitments to nonfamily members may produce feelings of insecurity and perhaps bewilderment on the part of husbands. The result may be strain or even resentment. For example, a wife may change her expectations and attitudes earlier or faster than her husband, or a husband may find he needs to take time out from his job to meet new family responsibilities. At the same time, some men may welcome the opportunity to share the burden of family support with their wives and the chance to spend more time with their children. Because the working woman cannot herself meet all of the requirements of house, children, and job, husbands may find themselves becoming steadily more involved in home and family.

The implications of this for male employment and life styles are unclear. Will men come to turn down overtime, refuse travel, and reject transfers because of the work commitment of their wives and the needs of their children? If males are able to share the burden of family support and develop the ability to express their feelings and emotions more openly, will male mortality fall? The implications of the rising rate of female employment on the lives of males have yet to be fully explored. But the reaction of men to the greater participation by women in the world outside the home will be an important determinant of how rapidly and how smoothly the change in sex roles occurs, and how society ultimately judges this evolution.

In summary, it is clear that married couples face new opportunities and new pressures as women's involvement in market work increases. These changes are likely to have a destabilizing impact on marriage, to improve the intrafamily bargaining power and rights of wives, and to unsettle the lives of husbands. Most importantly, as women take on new responsibilities outside of the home, they will of necessity devote less time to housework and child care. To date, there is no evidence that men have moved toward any meaningful sharing of these tasks. A critical issue, then, is what will happen to children in a society where a large proportion of the adult population is committed to activities outside of the home.

The Future of Parenthood

CHILD CARE ARRANGEMENTS OF WORKING MOTHERS

Although the total number of children under age eighteen in the United States has been declining due to the falling birth rate, the number of children with working mothers has been increasing rapidly. Forty-four percent of mothers were employed in 1973, as compared to 34 percent in 1964 and 22 percent in 1950. Mothers of older children are even more likely to work— 53 percent of women with school-age children worked in 1973— although one-third of the mothers of preschool children were employed as well. In fact, the number of preschool children with working mothers has increased by more than one-third in the last decade.

The arrangements which working parents make for the care of their children vary widely. Although the proportion of children in day care centers doubled between 1965 and 1970, these centers still provide for only 10 percent of all the preschool children of working mothers. The remaining nine out of ten children are cared for informally—some in their own homes by a father, a sibling or other relative, or a paid worker; some in the home of a family day care worker.

Most of the family day care workers who take in children are themselves mothers who care for only a few children at a time. They choose this work so that they can stay home with their families while earning some money, and to provide company for themselves and their children as well. Parental satisfaction with these informal arrangements has been found to be high, despite the fact that only 1 or 2 percent of these homes are estimated to be licensed. The quality of care offered undoubtedly varies widely.

Since there were an estimated six million children under age six who required some sort of child care in 1972, and only about one million were cared for in day care centers or licensed homes, there has been some pressure for the federal government to provide day care services on a greatly expanded basis. At least three different groups support an expanded government role in this area. One group consists of women who believe that their opportunities or their ability to cope with the dual responsibilities of home and job are limited by a lack of day care facilities. Another group is concerned about the early environment of children, and has argued that quality child care can enhance child development and provide greater equality of opportunity for children from poor families. Finally, there is a group that argues for day care programs which will enable poor women who head families to work, thus reducing welfare costs.

Since quality day care is labor-intensive and expensive, especially if an emphasis is placed on child development rather than merely custodial care, the question of who should pay and how much they should pay has been frequently debated. With the exception of the most affluent families, parents are currently allowed a tax deduction for child care expenses, and most proposals would extend this principle by providing a sliding fee schedule with free or very low cost services to poor families.

CONSEQUENCES FOR CHILDREN

Much of the controversy over whether women should work or not centers around the question of whether or not children will be adversely affected if mothers delegate child care to other persons while they are at work.

One reason for the fear that maternal employment harms children lies in early research on young children separated from their mothers for long periods or placed in institutions. The severe deprivation of attention and stimulation that these children suffer tends to produce intellectual retardation and social apathy or unresponsiveness. These effects have been extrapolated to suggest that the children of working women will not develop adequately. However, the separation of mother and child for routine, brief, nontraumatic periods does not seem to be harmful if adequate substitute care is provided. Indeed, a number of studies have suggested that the children of employed women compare favorably with the children of nonemployed women.

A more precise answer than this is not possible without specifying more carefully what *type of behavior* on the part of children is likely to be affected by a mother's employment and the total *circumstances* surrounding her employment. A review of several studies on these questions are illustrative.

Several early studies explored the presumed association between maternal employment and juvenile delinquency. They found that boys from lower-income families who were inadequately supervised were more likely to be delinquents, and that the sons of employed women were more likely to be inadequately supervised. But it was the quality of supervision rather than employment *per se* which contributed to delinquency. In general, these early reports linking juvenile delinquency to maternal employment have subsequently been qualified, as researchers have taken into account such critical factors as how the children were cared for in the mother's absence, the socioeconomic group being studied, and the emotional health of the family.

Children of working women have often been assumed to do poorly in school because their mothers have less time and energy to help their children with homework and other intellectual pursuits and may be disinterested in, or even rejecting of, their children. However, the children of working women do not seem to suffer impaired academic performance. Several studies have found a positive relationship between I.Q. scores and maternal employment. One study found that middle class sons of working women received lower grades than those with nonworking mothers. In the lower class, maternal employment is positively associated with academic performance among both sexes.

Children of working women have been found to be slightly higher in achievement motivation and to be more likely to plan to attend college. These effects are slight, however, and researchers have often failed to apply appropriate controls. For example, college aspirations may be linked to maternal employment because mothers are working to pay for tuition or because children from two-income families perceive college as economically feasible. As subsequent discussion indicates, employed mothers seem to provide their children, especially their daughters, with achievement models. As one might expect, then, college-educated daughters of employed mothers have higher career aspirations and achievements than the daughters of nonemployed mothers.

Employed mothers also tend to stress independence in their children. The children of working mothers typically have more household responsibilities than the children of full-time home-makers. But this stress on independence appears to be less true among well-educated women and women who enjoy their work. The latter seem to compensate for their employment by being especially nurturant toward their young children.

The natural maturation of the child may hold less threat for a woman with alternative satisfactions and commitments than for a mother who has invested all her time in home and family. Betty Friedan decries the softness and passivity of children raised by full-time housewives who are living vicariously through their children. She argues that the child of a woman with a sense of self, with interests and a life of her own, will be a stronger and more resilient adult. A study by M.R. Yarrow *et al.*, illuminates this point. Mothers were divided into four groups: satisifed homemak-ers, dissatisfied homemakers, satisfied employed women, and dis-satisfied employed women. Satisfied homemakers scored highest on a measure of adequacy of mothering. Dissatisfied mothers, whether working or not, scored lower, especially the dissatisfied homemaker. Those women who stressed duty as the reason for being a full-time homemaker had the very lowest scores on moth-ering. One can speculate that the children of dissatisfied home-makers would be better off if their mothers were employed.

The Yarrow study illustrates the importance of considering la-bor force participation as something more than a simple em-ployed/nonemployed dichotomy. The woman's motivation for working, her satisfaction with her job, the duration of employ-ment, her husband's opinion of her employment, the adequacy of child care, help received with housework, and socioeconomic sta-tus all seem likely to influence the consequences of maternal em-ployment for children. Further study should control for these dif-ferences. In addition, the date when a study was conducted can affect the results. Research on women who worked during the 1950s, when public opinion generally held that women should be home with their children, may not apply to the 1970s. Finally, little attempt has been made to relate the longer-term achieve-ments and mental health of children, as they are revealed over the life cycle of the child, with earlier influences, including the mother's employment. Until more research is done on this vital and complex question, it is difficult to come to any firm conclu-sions.

SEX ROLE ATTITUDES

Whatever the effects of a mother's employment on her children's welfare, the transmission of attitudes or values from one generation to the next is likely to be affected by the life styles of today's parents. In this regard, one interesting set of research findings shows that the children of employed mothers have a different concept of women's role than those whose mothers do not work. Several studies illustrate this point.

In a study by Philip Goldberg, college students were presented with short professional articles on topics ranging from city planning and law to art history and dietetics. In some cases, a particular article was attributed to a female author and in other cases to a male author. In every instance, students evaluating the quality of the work rated the manuscripts attributed to male authors higher than the manuscripts attributed to female authors, whatever the topic. These findings were later qualified by a replication of the original study by G.K. Baruch, which showed that the daughters of *employed* women were significantly less likely to devalue the articles attributed to women than were the daughters of full-time housewives.

Another group of researchers (Inge Broverman *et al.*) studied sex-role stereotypes in an attempt to learn which traits are seen as appropriately masculine and feminine. They developed a list of characteristics, such as "active" and "dependent," and asked samples of men and women to evaluate which traits typify males and which typify females. Typically male traits tended to reflect competency (independent, objective, active, competitive, logical, etc.) while female traits tended to form a warmth and expressiveness cluster (gentle, sensitive, tactful, religious, etc.). When describing themselves, women conformed to the female stereotype, even to the point of saying that they themselves were more passive and less rational and competent than men, as well as more warm and expressive. Daughters of employed women were expected to have a different view of women, however. The authors reasoned that:

> A person's perception of societal sex roles, and of the self in this context, may be influenced by the degree of actual role differentiation that one experiences in one's own family. Maternal employment status appears to be central to the role differentiation that occurs be-

tween parents. If the father is employed outside the home while the mother remains a full-time homemaker, their roles tend to be clearly polarized for the child. But if both parents are employed outside the home, their roles are more likely to be perceived as similar—not only because the mother is employed, but also because the father is more likely to share childrearing and other family-related activities.

Daughters of working women did indeed perceive significantly smaller differences between males and females relative to daughters of nonemployed women. In addition, while they did not differ from daughters of nonemployed women in describing women as warm and expressive, they did differ in that they described women as being relatively more competent. And sons of working women perceived less difference between men and women in their warmth and expressiveness. What these findings imply, of course, is that new experiences tend to generate new attitudes which may significantly influence the sex role behavior of the next generation of adults. And this interaction between experiences and attitudes can become a powerful basis for a cumulative movement toward more equality in the future. In the past, attitudes and experiences tended to reinforce one another to create a kind of cumulative inertia, but once the system has been perturbed, any return to the previous status quo is quite unlikely.

Some of the research on sex role attitudes has shown that boys as well as girls are influenced by the example set by a working mother. This is significant for, as we have seen, one area where the status quo appears to be rather firmly entrenched is in the amount of household work—including child care—which husbands are willing to undertake. But if young boys are growing up with a different set of attitudes than their fathers, the current situation could change.

If women continue to move into the labor force and a greater sharing of domestic responsibilities does not come about, then there are two other possible outcomes. One is a much greater delegation of child care and other personal services to public or private institutions outside of the family. Another is that families will simply have fewer children. Just as employed women have cut back on the number of hours they devote to housework so, too, they may choose smaller families to accommodate their need to supplement the family income or their new interest in careers outside the home.

EMPLOYMENT AND FAMILY SIZE

Raising children and being employed are both extremely demanding in terms of time and energy. Women involved in both activities at the same time find themselves stretched and drained to the point that they may wonder whether they are succeeding at either role. In fact, work overload is such a serious problem for the mothers of small children that most mothers of preschoolers do not work. Women with large families are also much less likely to work than mothers who have small families. The association between labor force participation and small families has been consistently documented, and is illustrated in the following Census Bureau data for ever-married women aged thirty-five to forty-four in 1974: nonemployed women had an average of 3.3 children; women employed part-time had an average of 3.1 children; and women employed full-time had an average of 2.8 children. Moreover, when asked about how many children they would like to have, or what they consider the ideal family size to be, women who work outside the home mention fewer numbers of children than other women.

A variety of factors have been suggested to explain the association between female employment and small families. For one, women who are unable to have children may find compensating satisfactions in a job or career. Alternatively, women who enjoy working may deliberately limit their family size to enable them to work. Working may fulfill needs for self-expression, creativity, accomplishment, and social identity that childbearing has previously satisfied. In addition, the cost of having a child is substantial, especially if a couple adds in the value of the wages that a full-time homemaker could be earning in the paid market place. Ritchie Reed and Susan McIntosh have calculated the cost of rearing a single child through college by adding the value of the wife's foregone earnings to an estimate of $33,000 for direct costs such as food and medical care. This cost totals $84,000 for a woman with an elementary school education, $99,000 for a woman with a high school degree, $122,000 for a woman with some college or a four-year degree, and $143,000 for a woman with five or more years of college. Second children are a bargain by comparison since they simply lengthen the time the mother spends out of the labor force, with the extra cost depending on how closely they are spaced. The cost of having a second child spaced two years later is, respectively, $47,000, $49,000, $53,000, and $56,000.

Clearly, the cost of not working is highest for well-educated women and this may be one reason better-educated women have smaller families. However, there are other factors that explain why such women limit their family size. The kinds of jobs they are likely to hold are relatively interesting, pleasant, and stimulating, compared with the opportunities available to unskilled women. In addition, they are more likely to be effective contraceptive users.

While the association between a woman's education and family size has been consistently documented, and many reasons have been posed to explain the relationship, the cause of the relationship is unclear. Do women have small families because they *wish* to work or *need* to work? Or do they have small families for other reasons and then find that they simply have more time to work? If a significant number of women are limiting their fertility because of the practical difficulties of combining motherhood with work, then increased availability of day care facilities and participation of husbands in housework and child care could reduce the barriers to childbearing on the part of women and bring about a rise in fertility. If, on the other hand, women who work have smaller families because working satisfies needs that they would otherwise meet by having babies, then it is unlikely that changes in day care and in the division of labor between husbands and wives will affect the birth rate. Linda Waite and Ross Stolzenberg have argued that women develop their plans for employment and childbearing jointly and simultaneously—that is, plans for working affect plans for having children and vice versa. They find that there is a reciprocal causation, but that women's employment plans have a somewhat greater influence on fertility than fertility has on employment plans. If this is so, it is an important finding.

If women's employment plans are an important determinant of family size, and if women's participation in the labor market continues to increase, the current fertility rate which is already at an all-time low may drop still further. The provision of more social supports, such as day care, could modify this conclusion by enabling women to combine work and family responsibilities more easily. But this latter argument also assumes that new attitudes which are emerging concerning both women's roles and the state of the economy and the environment will not change people's preferences about the desirability of children relative to other possible uses of scarce time and resources.

Many families may continue to have strongly positive feelings about children but may be forced to curtail childbearing so that wives can contribute to family income. Having a second earner in the family often makes the difference between just getting by and establishing a solid position within the ranks of the middle class. Thus, it may become increasingly difficult for women to *choose* to stay home and to forego the standard of living that two-career families can achieve. Americans have always judged their economic well-being not by the *absolute* value of their income but by their position *relative* to other families in the income structure. If most families have two incomes, those families with one earner may feel disadvantaged by comparison. It is difficult enough to keep up with the Joneses under normal circumstances but when both Joneses are working it is almost impossible. This brings us, then, to still another interesting question about the future: what will happen to the distribution of family income if more and more women choose, or feel required, to work?

Changes in the Distribution of Family Income

Although real incomes and standards of living have risen quite dramatically over the past three decades, the distribution of income among families has hardly changed at all. In 1972, for example, the 20 percent of families at the top of the income pyramid received slightly more than two-fifths of aggregate family income while the 20 percent at the bottom received only 5 percent. A similar picture has held since the end of World War II.

How does the participation of women in the labor force affect the income distribution of families? If all wives worked and women had the same earning potential as men, the answer would depend only on who married whom. A tendency for high-income men to marry high-income women would exacerbate the degree of income inequality relative to a world in which only husbands worked.

At present, the fact that less than half of all wives work complicates the analysis because the labor force participation of women tends to be negatively related to their husband's income but positively related to their own earnings prospects. The net result is that the labor force participation of wives increases as husband's earnings rise, up to the average earnings for all husbands, but then falls again at higher levels. Overall, this causes the current distribution of income to be somewhat more equal than it would be if wives did not work at all. Moreover, according to Lester Thurow, the increased participation of women in the labor force over the past twenty-five years has tended to reduce the relative inequality of family income. The stability in the overall distribution noted above evidently reflects the offsetting influences of other factors which, in the absence of more wives going to work, would have led to greater inequality. So the desire to keep up with the Joneses and to reduce disparities in income may indeed have been a potent force in bringing more women into paid employment.

An example to how this phenomenon has worked in the past is provided by an analysis of income differentials between black and white families. Because a greater proportion of black wives has traditionally been in the labor force, differences in the income status of black and white families have not been as great as the racial inequality in individual earnings. More recently, however, the labor force participation rate of white wives has surpassed that of black wives for the first time, causing some decline in the relative income position of black families.

This recent development may be a harbinger of greater inequality in the family income distribution generally. If there is an influx of relatively well-educated, high-earning women into the labor force—women who in the past have married well and worked less frequently than wives in lower income families—then greater inequality would ensue in the future. If this occurs, people might react with demands for new, more egalitarian tax policies to offset the greater dispersion in standards of living.

Conclusions and Policy Implications

In most of the preceding sections, no explicit attention has been given to the policy issues raised by the changes being reviewed here. But these questions are lurking just below the surface of the discussion.

Clearly, the potentially profound repercussions on home and family life which women's greater work attachment may bring will necessitate a rethinking of public policies in such diverse areas as social security, divorce, alimony, child support, welfare, and income tax laws. Many of these laws were based on the assumption that the vast majority of women were homemakers who were financially dependent on their husbands. Such laws will need to be retailored to fit a world in which that assumption is false at least as often as it is true. Already, working wives are pressing for a revision of Social Security and income tax laws which discriminate against two-earner families. But if they succeed someone else will have to bear the cost. And we may yet see a backlash if highly paid men and women pool income through marriage and exacerbate the disparities in family income.

Women's market participation also has implications for fertility and marital stability which will themselves change the shape of the future. For example, we have seen that improvements in women's economic opportunities appear to be a significant factor in rising divorce rates, currently the highest in the nation's history and in the industrialized Western world. This has contributed to an unprecedented increase in female-headed families. Indeed, the absolute increase in the number of children living in single-parent homes has exceeded the increase in the number living in two-parent homes over the decade of the sixties—a development that is in part an indictment of our welfare system, which recent research suggests contributes to the growth of single-parent homes. But given the size of this population and the poverty they often face, there is a need to reevaluate present alimony and child support laws. Fragmentary statistical evidence suggests these laws are working poorly indeed. Reform might entail designing a national child support policy establishing a fund to which all absent parents would contribute and from which all eligible children would draw; or, it might take the form of a system of divorce insurance, an idea which the New York State legislature is already considering.

While these are all important questions, the most critical issue has to do with the way in which the essential work of the household sector, especially child care, can be organized as women move increasingly into the labor market. The possibilities run the gamut from wholly private nonmarket arrangements, through increasing market organization, to substantial public involvement in the financing and providing of services. Will husbands and wives work out a new division of labor on a voluntary partnership basis? There is agitation for this on the part of many women, but as we have suggested, the overall record on male-female sharing of home tasks has not been reassuring. It is not clear whether the current lack of sharing is the result of ingrained attitudes or the absence of appropriate financial incentives, but as these attitudes or incentives shift we may see new patterns of behavior in the future.

In the event that husband-wife sharing of home responsibilities does not come about soon, how will the work of the home sector get done? Will the private market continue to organize to carry out these functions, as it already has with capital goods for the home, paid domestic help, household maintenance organizations, and day care services? Before these private mechanisms can develop, will they be overtaken by plans to socialize household work and to pay some or all of its workers out of public funds? For example, is a trust fund for children through which all parents or all adults will pay for individual or group care for all children a possibility? Will public involvement go beyond the paying of people to do household tasks, and develop into large-scale direct provision of household services, with child care as the major component?

These are some of the policy issues to which we need to turn our attention. At the present time most individuals or couples are making their decisions and plans alone, with little counselling or social support. The rules are changing and the final outcome, as well as much about the intervening process, is unclear.

Few social scientists think the family is going to disappear. However, the lower fertility and increased labor force participation of women will almost certainly continue to change the personal rewards, power relationships, role expectations, and ultimately even the definition or prevalence of marriage. More research, discussion, and debate are needed if social scientists and government decision-makers are to plan intelligently for the future and individuals are to move confidently into that future.

Phyllis A. Wallace

6

Impact of Equal Employment Opportunity Laws

[Title VII] represents a flat and absolute prohibition against all sex discrimination in conditions of employment. It is not concerned with whether the discrimination is "invidious" or not. It outlaws all sex discrimination in the conditions of employment. It authorizes but a single exception to this statutory command of nondiscrimination and that is a narrow one which, to be upheld, requires a finding that is necessary to the safe and efficient operation of the business. Gilbert et al. v. General Electric Co., *1975.*

Introduction

The laws of the federal government prohibiting employment discrimination may eventually have their widest impact in the area of sex discrimination. Until the passage of Title VII of the Civil Rights Act of 1964 women had few legal weapons to attack occupational segregation. In fact, the legislative history pertaining to the addition of the word "sex" to section 703(a) of Title VII is meager. The amendment to prohibit discrimination in employment because of sex as well as race, color, religion, and national

A professor of the Sloan School of Management at M.I.T. PHYLLIS A. WALLACE *has been the author of many studies in economics and others on sex and minority discrimination. Dr. Wallace has been on a number of governmental advisory committees. She is presently a trustee of The Brookings Institution and a member of the Board of Directors of The State Street Bank and Trust Company.*

123

origin "was offered in a tongue-in-cheek manner with the intent to undermine the entire Act and assist in its defeat" (*Wetzel et al. v. Liberty Mutual Insurance Co.*, 1975).

By 1975 a significant body of administrative interpretations and case law had developed on issues of equal compensation, maternity leave and benefits, pension plans, fringe benefits, and other terms and conditions of employment of women. Many of the rulings were based on general principles that had been propounded for racial discrimination. For example, the Supreme Court in the landmark Title VII case (*Griggs v. Duke Power Co.*, March 1971) articulated the doctrine of adverse impact. It stated that Title VII looks to the "consequences" not the intent of an employer's action. If any action taken by an employer has an adverse impact on the employment opportunities of any group protected by the law, the burden rests on the employer to prove that his discriminatory behavior is a business necessity—*i.e.*, necessary to the safe and efficient operation of the business.

Issues such as state protective laws, maternity leave, and marital status required the promulgation of special guidelines to ensure equal opportunities for all persons employed or seeking employment without regard to sex. Major conflicts have developed over the past decade among the federal agencies responsible for compliance of laws treating sex discrimination in employment. With few exceptions either the prohibition against sex discrimination or the implementation of special regulations lagged considerably behind the efforts to reduce racial discrimination. Nevertheless, significant progress has occurred within a short span.

This chapter will examine some of the dynamics of the development of an equal employment opportunity delivery system for women workers. Since Title VII of the Civil Rights Act of 1964 is the most comprehensive in scope, the major focus of this chapter will be on the implementation of this law. After a review of the enforcement stance of the Equal Employment Opportunity Commission (EEOC) as reflected in the modifications of its guidelines on sex discrimination, we will examine one of the most controversial issues, seniority versus affirmative action. Back pay as an effective remedy for employment discrimination is then discussed. Two important consent decrees affecting women workers, the American Telephone and Telegraph (AT&T) case and that of the Bank of America are assessed. Some concerns are raised about sex discrimination in employment in higher education before we conclude this overview of a decade of equal employment opportunity laws. Given the array of interventions that have been developed over the past ten years to reduce sex discrimination in the labor market, one may be somewhat more optimistic about the next decade.

Equal Employment Opportunity Laws

There are four principal federal measures prohibiting employment discrimination on the basis of sex:

1. *The Equal Pay Act of 1963,* section 6(d) of the Fair Labor Standards Act of 1938 as amended, requires that employees performing equal work be paid equal wages, regardless of sex. The Act became effective in 1964 and its coverage was extended in 1972 to include previously exempted administrative, executive, professional, technical employees, and outside salespersons. State and local government employees are also now covered. Employers are required to give equal compensation to employees who perform equal work involving substantially equal skill, effort, and responsibility under similar working conditions in the same establishment. All three of the criteria, equal skill, effort, and responsibility must be met before a violation is found, but the enforcement agency, the Wage and Hour Division of the Department of Labor, has defined the criteria "such that equal does not mean identical" (Commission on Civil Rights, *To Eliminate Employment Discrimination*).

In 1974 the Supreme Court vigorously interpreted the mandate that women workers were entitled to the same wage scales as men performing the same job (*Corning Glass Works v. Brennan*). Since wages encompass all remuneration including fringe benefits which an employee receives from the employer, it is likely that many more complaints will be made concerning pension plans, insurance programs, and other fringe benefits. The specific exemptions from the Equal Pay Act of bona fide seniority systems and merit systems may become matters of great concern in the future to women workers in blue collar jobs and to the millions of women who are employed in the public sector.

2. *Title VII of the Civil Rights Act of 1964* as amended prohibits discrimination in compensation, all terms, conditions, and privileges of employment by employers, employment agencies, labor

organizations, and joint labor management committees, because of an individual's race, color, religion, sex, or national origin. The EEOC has the responsibility for administration of the law. Title VII is the most comprehensive employment discrimination statute since it includes a wide range of activities—hiring, training, referral, promotion, discharge, wages and salary, fringe benefits. The broad coverage under the 1972 amendment to Title VII includes state and local government, educational institutions, as well as employers with fifteen or more employees.

EEOC's *Guidelines on Sex Discrimination,* discussed below, affirms the principle that employment decisions must be based on individual capacities and not on characteristics generally attributed to a group. Since 1972 the EEOC has been empowered to bring civil action suits against persons (except for government agencies where the Justice Department may file suits) engaging in unlawful employment practices. Prior to that time, the EEOC filed friend of the court briefs in a number of suits brought by private parties. In addition Title VII provides for injunctive and affirmative relief by federal courts, and such affirmative action "may include, but is not limited to, reinstatement or hiring of employees, with or without back pay—or any other equitable relief."

3. *Executive Order 11246* signed in 1965 prohibited discrimination in employment on the basis of race, color, religion, or national origin by federal contractors including those working on federally-assisted construction projects. The Office of Federal Contract Compliance (OFCC) in the Department of Labor administers the executive order. The federal contractors were also required to take affirmative action to ensure equal employment opportunity. Each nonconstruction contractor with fifty or more employees and a government contract of $50,000 or more is required to prepare a written affirmative action plan applicable to each of its facilities. The affirmative action plan must include goals for improving the employment of underutilized groups and timetables for achieving these goals.

In the event of noncompliance, various sanctions are authorized. These include contract cancellation, termination, or suspension; debarment from future contracts; referral to the Department of Justice for court action, or to the EEOC for appropriate action under Title VII. These strong sanctions have rarely been imposed. There is considerable lack of uniformity in the implementation of this executive order since the Department of Labor has designated eleven federal agencies to act as compliance agencies for nonconstruction contractors.

The prohibition against sex discrimination was not added to the requirements of the executive order until 1967; Executive Order 11375 became effective in October 1968. Specific regulations for affirmative action plans and the establishment of goals and timetables for women employed by federal contractors, were not adopted until December 1971. These regulations known as Revised Order No. 4 introduced the requirement that contractors remedy the effects of past discrimination experienced by incumbent employees, the "affected class." OFCC's *Guidelines on Sex Discrimination* was issued in 1970 and is not consistent with the more stringent regulations on maternity leave and benefits, pension plans, and bona fide occupational requirements (BFOQ) in the 1972 guidelines of the EEOC. Proposed revisions by OFCC to bring their guidelines on sex discrimination into conformity with the EEOC's have met strenuous opposition.

4. *Title IX of the Education Amendments of 1972* forbids sex discrimination against students and employees in most educational programs or activities receiving federal financial assistance. Regulations aimed at equalizing opportunities for women in some 16,000 school systems and 2,700 colleges and universities went into effect on 21 July 1975. These educational institutions will be required to end discriminatory practices against women in school admissions, employment, financial aid, vocational and academic counseling, and athletics, or be cut-off from federal funding. While Title VI of the Civil Rights Act of 1964 applies broadly to discrimination in all federal funding, Title IX applies only to education. The Office of Civil Rights, Department of Health, Education, and Welfare, is responsible for enforcing Title IX regulations.

The employment provisions apply to recruitment, advertising, application for employment, hiring, upgrading, promotion, consideration for and award of tenure, transfer, demotion, layoff, compensation, job assignments, classifications and structure, fringe benefits, marital or parental status, and selection and financial support for training including professional meetings, conferences, and other related activities. The experience of the Department of Health, Education, and Welfare in implementing Executive Order 11246 (See *Higher Education Guidelines, Executive Order 11246.*) may have influenced its decision to shift its compliance activities from investigations of individual charges to broad, systemic forms of discrimination (New York *Times,* May 30, 1975). See discussion below on sex discrimination in employment in higher education.

Implementation of Equal Employment Legislation

The evolution of the Title VII law on sex discrimination in employment was retarded by the conflict over state protective laws, uncertainties over the meaning of the BFOQ provisions, and inconsistencies between the Equal Pay Act and Title VII. An analysis of the three versions of EEOC's *Guidelines on Discrimination Because of Sex* released in December 1965, August 1969, and April 1972 reveals significant changes in the administrative interpretations of the law. The Griggs decision stated that "great deference" would be shown to the interpretation of Title VII by the agency, EEOC, charged with its administration. The guidelines recommended an enforcement stance for state protective laws, BFOQ, fringe benefits, seniority systems, marital status, advertising, employment agencies, preemployment inquiries as to sex, the relationship of Title VII to the Equal Pay Act, and employment policies relating to pregnancy and childbirth. (See Appendix A for *Guidelines on Discrimination Because of Sex,* April 1972.)

The introduction to the 1965 guidelines stated:

> The Commission has proceeded with caution in interpreting the scope and application of Title VII's prohibition of discrimination in employment on account of sex . . . . An overly literal interpretation of the prohibition might disrupt longstanding employment practices required by state legislation or collective bargaining agreements without achieving compensating benefits in progress towards equal opportunity . . . .

STATE PROTECTIVE LAWS

At the beginning of the twentieth century, many states had enacted laws designed to protect women workers. The statutes regulated activities such as employment in certain occupations, working more than a specified number of hours or during certain hours of the night, and the lifting of heavy weights. Although much of the legislation was based on the belief that women workers needed special health, safety, and welfare protection, by the

1960s these laws were used to restrict the opportunities for women to expand their participation in the labor force.

The 1965 guidelines stated:

> The Commission does not believe that Congress intended to disturb such laws and regulations which are intended to, and have the effect of protecting women against exploitation and hazard. Accordingly, the Commission will consider limitations or prohibitions imposed by such state laws or regulations as a basis for application of the bona fide occupational qualification exception.

Within a short period of time EEOC found the task of harmonizing Title VII and state protective legislation so irreconcilable that it declined to consider cases involving state protective laws and advised complainants to litigate these issues (*Second Annual Report,* U.S. Equal Employment Opportunity Commission).

The 1969 revised guidelines on sex discrimination asserted that state protective laws would no longer be considered as bona fide occupational qualification exceptions:

> Accordingly, the Commission has concluded that such laws and regulations conflict with Title VII of the Civil Rights Act of 1964 and will not be considered a defense to an otherwise established unlawful employment practice as a basis for the application of the bona fide occupational qualification exception.

The 1972 guidelines stipulated "that such [protective] laws and regulations conflict with and are superseded by Title VII of the Civil Rights Act of 1964." By then, several courts had struck down state protective laws (*Rosenfeld v. Southern Pacific Company,* 1971; *Bowe v. Colgate-Palmolive,* 1969; and *Hays v. Potlach Forest, Inc.,* 1972).

BONA FIDE OCCUPATIONAL QUALIFICATION (BFOQ)

A limitation was placed on the proscription against sex discrimination through section 703 (e)(1) of Title VII which states that it was not an unlawful employment practice to employ, classify, refer, or train an individual on the basis of sex "where sex is a bona fide occupational qualification reasonably necessary to the normal operation of that particular business or enterprise." This BFOQ exception applies to religion and national origin but not race, and has been used mainly in sex discrimination. From the beginning EEOC endorsed a narrow interpretation of the bona fide occupational qualification exception as to sex. In response to a request from an airline on a written interpretation of sex as a BFOQ for the position of flight cabin attendants, the EEOC held a public hearing in September 1967. The Commission held that sex was not a bona fide occupational qualification for the position of flight attendant (February 1968). The three versions of the EEOC guidelines on sex discrimination in employment specified that the following situation did not warrant application of the BFOQ exception:

(1) The refusal to hire a woman because of her sex, based on assumptions of the comparative employment characteristics of women in general. For example, the assumption that the turnover rate among women is higher than among men. (2) The refusal to hire an individual based on stereotyped characterizations of the sexes. Such stereotypes include, for example, that men are less capable of assembling intricate equipment; that women are less capable of aggressive salesmanship. (3) The refusal to hire an individual because of the preferences of co-workers, the employer, clients or customer . . . .

The business necessity test is that the "essence of business operation would be undermined by not hiring members of one sex exclusively."

The courts have agreed with the narrow interpretation of the BFOQ exception and have ruled that the principle of nondiscrimination requires that individuals be considered on the basis of individual capacities and not on the basis of any characteristics generally attributed to the group (*Weeks v. Southern Bell Telephone,* 1969; *Sprogis v. United Air Lines,* 1971; *Diaz v. Pan American Airways, Inc.,* 1971). The Diaz case is interesting because the sex discrimination provisions were applied to males. The court held that customer preference for female flight attendants was not a BFOQ, and granted relief to a male plaintiff who had been refused employment. The *Phillips v. Martin Marietta Corp.,* 1971 decision by the Supreme Court appears to be indirectly related to BFOQ. The court held that an employer's policy of not hiring women with preschool age children although men with preschool age children were employed violated Title VII, but the court remanded the case for further consideration of whether the policy could be justified as BFOQ.

EQUAL PAY

Section 703(h) of Title VII specified that employers could legally differentiate upon the basis of sex in determining wages or compensation paid to employees if such differentiation was authorized by the Equal Pay Act of 1963. Under the Equal Pay Act employers were permitted to maintain wage differentials between men and women if the differentials were based on a merit system, a seniority system, a system measuring earnings by quantity or quality of production, or on any factor other than sex. Initially, the EEOC accepted the equal pay for equal work standards of the Equal Pay Act in determining unlawful sex discrimination in compensation under Title VII.

By 1969, however, the EEOC found "reasonable cause" to believe that certain wage differentials (especially fringe benefits) between male and female employees constituted unlawful sex discrimination under Title VII without respect to whether they were permissible under the Equal Pay Act. The 1972 guidelines indicated that where a defense based on the Equal Pay Act was raised under a Title VII proceeding, appropriate considerations would be given to interpretations from the Wage and Hour Division, Department of Labor, but the EEOC would not be bound by them.

FRINGE BENEFITS

A most severe conflict has developed between the interpretations of the Wage and Hour Administrator, OFCC, and the EEOC on the matter of fringe benefits. Under the Equal Pay Act wages are defined as all remuneration to employees including pension contribution and fringe benefits. The 1972 EEOC sex guidelines prohibited discrimination between men and women with regard to fringe benefits (medical, hospital, accident, life insurance and retirement benefits; profit sharing and bonus plans; leave and other terms and conditions and privileges of employment). Under EEOC guidelines the fact that the cost of a fringe benefit is greater for one sex than the other may not be used as a defense under a Title VII charge of sex discrimination. The EEOC's position that it is unlawful for an employer to differentiate in retirement benefits on the basis of sex, has embroiled the federal compliance agencies in a major controversy.

For almost two years OFCC attempted to revise the fringe benefit requirement of its sex guidelines to accord with the interpretations of EEOC. As of June 1975, the Secretary of Labor had not issued the extensively revised regulations. OFCC, however, did not recommend that employers be required to provide equal benefits. Instead it presented alternative options for comment; alternative A, equal benefits to be paid by employers for male and female employees, and alternative B, equal contributions. The controversy is over whether the actuarial tables used to determine the benefits of male and female annuitants sanction disparate treatment based on sex. The Teachers Insurance and Annuity Association of America—College Retirement Equities Fund (TIAA-CREF) indicated that equal benefits would prove costly since payments would not reflect differences in male and female longevity.

The issue of conflicting regulations on pension plans rose again when proposed regulations for Title IX for Higher Education were released by the Department of Health, Education, and Welfare. This agency followed OFCC's guidelines which allow employers to follow either equal contribution or equal benefits to members of each sex. Since there is a lack of consensus among the federal compliance agencies, the Equal Employment Coordinating Council has been requested to draft uniform pension benefits guidelines based on sex. This intergovernmental unit (EEOC, Department of Labor, Department of Justice, Civil Rights Commission, and Civil Service Commission) has failed in attempts to produce uniform guidelines in testing and on seniority. Eventually, the courts will have to decide on whether a uniform federal policy on sex discrimination in compensation should be based on interpretations under the Equal Pay Act or the interpretations under Title VII.

PREGNANCY

The major battle over employment restrictions due to pregnancy has developed mainly in the courts. Policies relating to pregnancy and childbirth were not included in the 1965 and 1969 versions of the EEOC guidelines. Under the 1972 guidelines, disabilities caused or contributed by pregnancy, miscarriage, abortion, childbirth, and recovery are, for all job-related purposes, temporary disabilities and should be treated as such under health or temporary disability insurance or sick leave plan.

The proposed revision in the OFCC's guidelines to conform with the policies of EEOC on pregnancy met great opposition from employers:

(1) Already women receive wage benefits for days of absence as a result of sickness and accident disabilities that are greatly disproportionate to the wage continuation benefits which men receive. Treating pregnancy as a sickness and accident disability no matter how brief the average period of such disability can only further distort this important benefit in favor of female employees. (AT&T)

(2) We are unable to agree with the apparent implication of the proposed guidelines that an insurance program such as ours discriminates against the more than 90,000 female employees of GM, either in fact or law. Rather, it would seem that our female employees are being advantaged due to their inherent femininity, not only by receiving disproportionate amounts of weekly benefits due to sickness or injury, but also by being eligible for and receiving up to six weeks' benefits because of pregnancy. (General Motors)

The Health Insurance Association of America and American Life Insurance Association commented on the cost to employers of following the proposed guidelines by OFCC:

With respect to hospital and medical expenses coverage under a typical health insurance plan, the additional cost to an employer to include a pregnancy benefit payable on the same basis as if it were an accident or sickness has been estimated to be about 5 to 10 percent of premium for basic accident and sickness coverage.

The policies of EEOC were upheld in six cases decided in 1975, and one class action suit, *Wetzel v. Liberty Mutual Insurance Company* will be argued in the Supreme Court during the 1975-76 term. The Third Circuit Court approved a lower court ruling that the policies of the insurance company of excluding pregnancy benefits from the company's income protection plan and requiring such employee to return to work within three months after childbirth or be terminated, discriminated against women in violation of Title VII.

In June 1975, *Gilbert et al. v. General Electric Company,* another class action suit that had the International Union of Electrical, Radio, and Machine Workers as one of the plaintiffs, upheld the guidelines of the EEOC. The Fourth Circuit Court affirmed the decision of the lower court that the General Electric Company

violated Title VII by excluding from coverage under its nonoccu-
pational sickness and accidents benefits program, pregnancy-
related disability benefits. The lawsuit was filed in 1972 by seven
female employees on behalf of the company's approximately
100,000 female employees.

Prior to the coverage of state and local government employees
under Title VII beginning in 1972, numerous cases dealing with
mandatory maternity leaves were filed by public school teachers.
These cases were decided under the Equal Protection clause of
the Fourteenth Amendment of the Constitution (*La Fleur v. Cleve-
land Board of Education, Cohen v. Chesterfield County School Board*).
However, the Supreme Court ruled in June 1974 that a decision
by California not to insure under the state disability benefits program, disability from normal pregnancy did not violate the Equal
Protection clause (*Geduldig v. Aiello*).

Seniority vs. Affirmative Action

The administrative rulings and the initiation of litigation on
sex discrimination occurred in periods of high levels of economic
activity. The deep and prolonged decline in economic activity
that started in the last quarter of 1973 was responsible for a shift
in the labor markets from emphasis on hiring and promoting to
layoffs. Within the climate of a prosperous economy equal employment opportunity focused on undertaking affirmative action
in order to remedy past discrimination. In 1975 circuit court decisions have resolved the apparent conflict between layoff procedures governed by reverse order of seniority as required by collective bargaining agreements and procedures designed to
maintain goals established under affirmative action programs. In
both cases black workers who had acquired little seniority as a
result of past discriminatory employment practices were laid off
first.

The last in first out (LIFO) procedures of layoff meant that a
disproportionate share of unemployment would be borne by
these more junior employees. These racial cases are important
because they may establish certain judicial precedents which the
courts will follow on sex discrimination cases. The impact of layoff may be less for women workers since they are concentrated in
clerical or service occupations in the nonunion sector. Where
women have been hired recently in so-called nontraditional jobs

such as working on the assembly line in an automobile plant or as a member of the regular police force, they will be vulnerable to layoffs because of their low seniority status.

In the *Jersey Central Power and Light Company v. IBEW Local Unions* case the district court ruled that a proposed layoff of four hundred employees be carried out in such a manner as to preserve the ratios of minorities and women of each group prior to the layoff. A conciliation agreement obligated the employer to use its "best efforts" to increase the percentages of minority groups and female employees in its work force over a five-year period to the percentages that these groups represented in the relevant labor markets. The union charged reverse discrimination, preferential treatment, and violation of seniority procedures stipulated in the collective bargaining agreement. The appellate court declared in January 1975 that a plant-wide seniority system that is facially neutral was not invalid under Title VII (was a bona fide seniority system) even if it continued the effect of past discrimination.

The first case on the seniority/affirmative action conflict was the *Watkins v. Steelworkers, Local 2369 and Continental Can Company*. A reduction in employment at a plant in accordance with reverse order of seniority had eliminated all except two blacks from the work force. Early in 1974 the Louisiana district court ordered the employer to recall enough blacks to restore the racial percentage that existed as of the date of the last new employee hired. If future layoffs were to be made, they were to be allocated between white and black employees so that the black/white ratio would remain unchanged. This ruling was reversed by the Fifth Circuit Court in July 1975. The appellate court held that regardless of an earlier history of employment discrimination, when present hiring practices are nondiscriminatory, an employer's use of a long-established seniority system to determine the order of layoff and recall of employees was not a violation of Title VII. Thus a practice which is facially neutral but results in the discharge of more blacks than whites to the point of eliminating blacks from the work force is held not prohibitive by Title VII.

Statistics on layoffs during the recession that started in the third quarter of 1973 revealed that the job loser pattern was dominated by industry attachment; the goods producing industries had more cutbacks than service industries. In absolute and relative terms men experienced greater job loss, though not a higher unemployment rate, than women. Women workers were in

service or trade industries or those occupations where there were
fewer layoffs ("Memorandum and Statistics Prepared for Secretary of Labor Dunlop by BLS Commissioner Shiskin On Job Los-
ers in the Current Recession," *Daily Labor Report* (no. 79), Bureau
of National Affairs, April 23, 1975).

One case, *Bales et al. v. General Motors,* that focused on affirmative action and seniority for women workers was postponed indefinitely. Eight women workers on the assembly line at a California plant of General Motors filed a class action suit, after all
481 female hourly production workers were laid off during a reduction in the work force. Since no women had been hired to do
assembly line work at this plant until 1968 (four years after the
passage of Title VII), they had acquired little seniority. Both the
employer and the union rejected the remedies proposed by these
workers—share the work, work alternate weeks, recall enough
women from layoff to give them the same proportion of jobs as
they had before the reduction in force, and work exchange between senior men and junior women. The union, the United Automobile Workers, suggested instead a "front pay" plan whereby
an employer in accordance with seniority provisions of a contract
might layoff an employee but would pay the employee for a period equal to time that the individual would have escaped layoff
had the company hired at the time (s)he originally applied.

Women account for about one-fifth of union members and are
concentrated in a small number of unions. A study by the Department of Labor showed that in those unions where workers
are heavily organized, women workers are a negligible proportion
of total employment. In five industries in which women make up
at least half of those employed, only two (apparel and comm-
munications) show a relatively high degree of organization. In
1974 women members of fifty-eight labor unions established a
national organization, The Coalition of Labor Union Women, "to
improve the lives of working women by becoming activists on
women's issues within their unions." The limited participation of
union women in nontraditional jobs may minimize the effect of
the seniority conflict with affirmative action plans. The oral arguments on the appeal of the Jersey Central case indicated that the
layoff did not create a disproportionate impact upon the percentage of women workers similar to that of minority group employees.

Layoffs in the public sector might not adversely affect women
since the major concentration of women in state and municipal

employment is in office and clerical and para-professional jobs. Within these merit systems length of service may be the criterion applied to determine who is retained. Since women now comprise more than two percent of the nation's police force and many work as patrol officers, they may bear a disproportionate share of any reduction in that work force. It was not until the 1972 amendment that police departments and other public employers were covered under Title VII. The Crime Control Act of 1973 also banned sex discrimination by recipients of federal aid to law enforcement agencies. In New York City 400 of the city's 618 women police officers were laid off. Most of them had been hired since 1973 (New York *Times,* August 12, 1975).

Reduction in the work force generated a number of debates on alternative strategies and the reduced work week was examined but not where the primary issue was affirmative action. Over two thousand telephone operators in New York City shifted to a four day week in order to protect the jobs of four hundred employees scheduled to be laid off. The company and union negotiated this arrangement in what appears to be a job function to be phased out as more sophisticated technology is substituted.

Unions have recommended the conversion from narrow departmental seniority lines to plant-wide seniority as an appropriate resolution to the seniority versus affirmative action conflict. In many industries jobs have been structured along sex lines and women workers have not been able to transfer into male departments or are not permitted to carry their seniority with them. The policy statement by the International Electrical Workers Union asserts that changing the seniority system to a plant-wide system will permit all employees to achieve their rightful place based upon their original date of hire.

The issue of retroactive seniority to individuals covered under Title VII will be argued in the Supreme Court in the fall term of 1975 (*Franks v. Bowman Transportation*). The EEOC and Department of Justice will seek a reversal of a lower court decision. Two blacks who were denied employment as over the road truck drivers seek to be awarded retroactive seniority relief. The appeals court held that Title VII precluded an award of seniority relief to previously rejected applicants. A seniority system based on date of actual employment is by definition a bona fide seniority system within the meaning of section 703(h). The *Franks v. Bowman* case was more narrowly defined then the usual LIFO cases.

Back Pay

The courts have broad remedial powers to prescribe effective relief once a violation of Title VII has been established. The federal compliance agencies have argued and the courts have upheld in numerous cases that victims of job discrimination should be "made whole"—"*i.e.*, restored to a position where they would be were it not for the unlawful discrimination." Back pay fulfills the central statutory purposes of Title VII of eradicating discrimination and making persons whole for injuries suffered through past discrimination. (Back pay may be assessed for not more than two years prior to filing of a charge with EEOC or longer than two years prior to filing of an individual complaint or the issuance of a letter finding after a compliance reveiw by OFCC.) The Supreme Court noted in the case of *Albemarle Paper Company et al. v. Moody*, 1975, that the back pay provision of Title VII was expressly modeled on the back pay provision of the Taft-Hartley Act and it may be assumed that Congress was aware that the NLRB awards back pay as a matter of course—"not randomly or in the exercise of a standardless discretion, and not merely where employer violations are peculiarly deliberate, egregious, or inexcusable."

This recent decision clarified the right to back pay on an issue of racial discrimination and should strengthen future efforts of women workers to be made whole. Women had won significant back pay awards through litigation and also through negotiated settlements. In an Equal Pay Act suit brought against the General Electric Company by the International Union of Electrical Workers, 350 women at an Indiana facility of the company were granted $300,000 in back pay and an additional $250,000 in higher wages annually. The union charged that the company had paid female employees less than males doing comparable work in twenty-one job categories, and that the company maintained two separate classifications for each of these jobs, one filled predominately by males and the other by females. In each case the male classification was more highly paid, with the differentials ranging up to 94.5 cents an hour.

The AT&T consent decree of January 1973 was the largest back pay settlement ever made. AT&T and its twenty-four subsidiary operating companies, the largest employer in the country, agreed to pay approximately $7.5 million mainly to three thousand women in craft jobs. A year later, $7 million back pay was ordered to women in low level management jobs. The wage adjustments for those women and minorities who never sought promotions because they were aware of the company's discriminatory practices total more than $30 million, and a $23 million wage adjustment was agreed to under the consent decree covering first level managers.

The AT&T Case

The impact of the AT&T case will be enormous not because of these monetary awards, but because it represented the first effort to deal with every aspect of employment discrimination on a comprehensive basis. The federal compliance agencies (EEOC, Department of Labor, and Justice) developed a cohesive strategy that coordinated equal pay, seniority, upgrading and transfer, affirmative action goals and timetables, back pay, and pay adjustments. The mix of strategies for resolution of the problems included adminstrative litigation, negotiated settlement, and implementation of consent decrees.

The AT&T and federal compliance agencies agreed in a consent decree signed in January 1973 that an affirmative action plan incorporating goals for achieving full utilization of women and minorities at all levels of management and nonmanagement would be implemented over a six-year period. In the more than six hundred Bell System establishments with nearly a million workers, nearly three-fifths of whom were women, greater mobility would be ensured through the operation of an upgrading and transfer plan for nonmanagement job changes. The net credited service or seniority for purposes of transfer and promotion was expanded to mean length of service with the operating company instead of within a department or unit. A central transfer bureau would inform nonmanagement employees of prospective job opportunities. Although the pay adjustments in this case were the largest ever made, the cost of restructuring transfer and promotion systems and revamping personnel and industrial relations systems may total millions of dollars (Phyllis A. Wallace, ed., *Equal Employment Opportunity and the AT&T Case*).

After signing of the first telephone consent decree both the federal government and AT&T institutionalized more effective procedures for handling equal employment opportunity issues. The 1973 consent decree was amended in 1975. Since AT&T had not met the first year goals in many job classifications, the supplemental agreement required the company to give priority treatment to women and minorities in hiring and promotion. The number of priority placements among the affected individuals should equal 50 percent of the deficiencies in meeting employment objectives or half of the projected job opportunities for the quarter, whichever is smaller. The "frontloading" of individuals in the deficient categories should permit a reduction of 1973 shortfalls in meeting some of the targets for employees in nontraditional jobs.

In addition, specified sums ranging from $125 to $1,500 will be paid to employees who would have contributed to the reduction of the employment deficiencies in 1973 had appropriate personnel action of either promotion or hiring been undertaken. Each operating company will contribute on a *pro-rata* basis to a Bell System Affirmative Action Fund to be used for the special payments as well as for such special programs as: 1) studies designed to examine equipment used in craft positions which has been an obstacle to the performance of women in these jobs; 2) programs to determine technical skills and knowledge required for second and third level management jobs and to develop courses to enable such persons to move from nontechnical management jobs to technical management jobs; 3) identification and the establishment of contracts with special interest groups with expertise in recruiting and referring minorities and women; 4) feasibility study on the value of Awareness Training Program Packages for supervision of women and minority managers (*Supplemental Agreement, Equal Employment Opportunity Commission et al. v. AT&T*).

The monitoring mechanism that represented a joint effort of the federal compliance agencies and the company was developed and made on-site reviews of twenty-three Bell System companies. While the 1973 intermediate targets for allocations of job opportunities by sex, race, or ethnic groups were not met in many companies, the system-wide operating companies did achieve more than 90 percent of their 1974 intermediate targets. During the combined 1973-74 period women managers at the second level and above, increased by 46 percent and women in craft jobs increased by 119 percent. Such a detailed implementation of an affirmative action plan should be examined carefully for its utility and/or replicability in other industries.

TABLE 1. AFFIRMATIVE ACTION IN THE BELL SYSTEM, 1973-74

	Profile		Net gain in
	1/1/73	*12/31/74*	*1973 & 74*
Women, Second level management and above	5,168	7,570	2,402
Women, Craft jobs	6,407	14,032	7,625

Source: Supplemental AT&T Agreement, May 13, 1975.

Bank of America, San Francisco

In July 1974 a consent decree signed in a federal court in San Francisco settled a class-action suit (*Wells v. Bank of America,* 1974) that had been filed by several women in the international division of the Bank of America. The bank was charged with having discriminated against women with respect to recruitment, hiring, training, and promotion for managerial positions and overseas assignments. The settlement included the establishment of a five-year program of goals and timetables for the employment of women as bank officers and it also included goals for management training programs. A $3,750 million affirmative action trust fund was established by the bank to be funded in the manner shown in Table 2.

TABLE 2. BANK OF AMERICA AFFIRMATIVE ACTION TRUST FUND

Self-Development Trust	$ 850,000
Women Employees Trust	850,000
Management Training & Special Development Trusts	1,750,000
Other Payments	36,000
Attorney Fees	250,000

Source: Daily Labor Report, July 1975.

The trust funds were initally hailed as an alternative to back pay as a remedy for past discrimination but nearly a year later the federal judge who had approved the original settlement ordered the company to stop payments under the Self-Development Trust. Over a three-year period the management training program should benefit as many as six-hundred women college graduates employed by the bank in nonmanagement capacities who will be promoted after the completion of their training. Thus, the primary objective of the consent decree has not been undermined.

Higher Education

Sex discrimination in employment in the institutions of higher education emerged in the 1970s as a major battleground of confrontation. Since the Equal Pay Act had exempted administrative and professional and executive workers and Title VII had initially excluded educational institutions, women seeking to remedy discrimination in higher education found little leverage in the federal laws in the 1960s. Executive Order 11246 as amended to include sex discrimination did not become effective until late in 1968. However, in 1970 several groups representing women filed more than 360 class-action complaints against institutions of higher education which were federal contractors. By 1975, major changes were made in the equal employment opportunity delivery systems in this area—amendment of Title VII to include educational institutions (1972), passage of Title IX of Educational Amendment of 1972, release of affirmative action guidelines for colleges and universities by HEW (1972), and modifications in EEOC's guidelines on sex discrimination (1972).

The internal labor market of academic employers is divided into an administrative and a managerial segment, support staff including both blue- and white-collar workers, and faculty. In large research-teaching universities, a professional staff may also be present. These nonfaculty members may be primarily engaged in research activities. However, the controversy has involved mainly that segment of the educational labor market that deals with faculty. Disputes over wage discrimination and terms and conditions of employment have generated heated debate. Much of the confusion stems from the major conflict between federal compliance agencies over the responsibility for assessing employment in academic institutions. The Carnegie Commission on Higher Education noted that

> Higher education long ago in keeping with its own principles of finding merit wherever it could be found and rewarding it, should have been searching more actively for merit among women and minori-

ties. . . . It has failed its own principles and impoverished its own performance by the neglect of large pools of potential academic competence. It has looked for merit mostly within 40 percent of the population—white males—and largely neglected the other 60 percent. (New York *Times*, August 11, 1975)

Conclusions

The Congress and the administrative agencies responsible for implementation of equal employment opportunity laws and the courts have perceived sex discrimination as less invidious than other types of employment discrimination. During the past decade women have exercised their rights under Title VII to make it more meaningful. Large numbers of women workers had to resort to filing charges alleging discrimination when other grievance procedures of the work place failed. In its first year of operation, approximately two thousand complaints charged sex discrimination and by fiscal year 1973 about 34,000 such complaints were filed (see Table 3). Even though close to 15 percent of the sex charges were filed by male workers, this category of complaint accounted for about two-fifths of all charges of employment discrimination before EEOC. In a hearing before the Joint Economic Committee of the Congress in 1973 the Chairman of EEOC noted that 122 court cases had been filed since the 1972 amendment to Title VII that enabled the Commission to enforce the law by going to court. Allegations of discrimination because of sex accounted for about half of the complaints.

TABLE 3. EEOC—SEX DISCRIMINATION CHARGES, 1973

Respondent	Female	Male	Total
Private Employers	20,108	3,646	23,754
State and Local Government	2,257	241	2,498
Educational Institutions	1,041	97	1,138
Apprenticeship Committee	170	9	118
Employment Agencies	519	402	921
Union	341	70	411
Labor-Management	2,786	338	3,124
Other Multiple Respondents	1,768	172	1,940

Source: Eighth Annual Report, U. S. Equal Employment Opportunity Commission, Washington, D.C., 1974.

This review of a decade of implementation of equal employment opportunity laws dealing with sex discrimination reveals how difficult it is to effect change in the institutional behavior of employers, unions, educational institutions, and administrative agencies. Despite the substantial cost of noncompliance (particularly in class action suits, back pay awards, and other affirmative action remedies), enforcement of these laws has been uneven. Because of the lag of including sex discrimination under Executive Order 11246 and the unresolved early conflict between Title VII and state protective laws, sex discrimination did not receive much attention before 1970.

The number of agencies with responsibilities for enforcing provisions of laws prohibiting sex discrimination has increased as the number of federally assisted programs has expanded. Thus, the Comprehensive Health Manpower Act of 1971 and the Nurse Training Act of 1971, Title IX of the Education Amendments of 1972, Law Enforcement Assistance Act, and the General Revenue Sharing include compliance responsibilities to recipients of federal funds. These federal laws along with state and local regulations on fair employment practices, including sex discrimination, expand the protection for women workers in a variety of industries and occupations. Unfortunately, there is a lack of uniformity among the federal agencies on the minimum standards for the federal assistance activities.

There have been few attempts to estimate the impact on the employment of women of the equal employment opportunity laws. In a 1973 report prepared for the EEOC, Orley Ashenfelter and James Heckman estimated the rate of change between 1966 and 1970. Using data from 40,445 establishments reporting to the EEOC in both years, they noted that the occupational distribution of white women had changed very little relative to the occupational distribution of white males. If these 1966-70 rates of change were maintained indefinitely, it would require eleven and twenty-four years, respectively, for black and Spanish women to achieve the same occupational position as white females. Such a comparison of the occupational position of minority women and white women, however, is dangerous as Barbara Reagan has noted. Indeed, Reagan hypothesizes that if the 1966-70 rate of change continues indefinitely, after black and Spanish women reach the occupational position of Anglo (non-Hispanic) women in the predicted eleven and twenty-four years, similar resistance to entry to higher pay levels will set in and they will be slowly pushed back (Reagan, *Comments on Ashenfelter-Heckman Paper, MIT, Research Workshop on Equal Employment Opportunity,* 1974).

Future Prospects

Although individual complaints may provide an opportunity for compliance agencies to investigate employment practices of employers, unions, or employment agencies, the labor market options of women will be enhanced in the future through a better perception of "institutionalized sex discrimination." The operational definition of employment discrimination that has been incorporated into the body of case law on equal employment opportunity focuses on the differential results from the functioning of the labor market. The data base to-date relies heavily on racial discrimination cases.

We are just beginning to understand some of the interactions (psychological, economic, legal) of a very complex social system. The other chapters in this volume have noted that a long period of transition and of adjustment is necessary, but that the dynamic and cumulative interaction between expectations and behavior of women in the home and in the marketplace will move them toward greater equality. The economic environment may prove to be the major determinant of women's role in the 1980s. Will a scarcity of jobs in the next decade produce greater competition in the labor market and a tremendous backlash against women?

Martha W. Griffiths

7

Requisites for Equality

As the move toward equality between the sexes gains momentum it is well to remember that the movement is old, and that it is not indigenous to this country. For a long time women have wondered why they and they alone feed, bathe, and diaper the baby; why they arise before the sun to prepare the meals, and continue through the evening in order to do the dishes, put the children to bed, and turn down the covers for a husband still reading the paper in the room below. It is an error to assume that some strong person—parent, guardian, in-law, or government—can reach into the home and change this established order. In fact, no one can pass an enforceable law which will apportion the care of a child between parents, or the scrubbing of clothes between husband and wife. No unprejudiced, nonbiased policeman or judge can be assigned to the home for twenty-four hour duty. The way to equality is not only simpler, it is more logical, and within the reach of American women today.

Women have the right to vote. They must learn to use it for themselves rather than being distracted by highly idealistic slogans such as "peace in our time," "food for the hungry world" or other equally worthy pleas; to vote for those men and women

MARTHA W. GRIFFITHS *is a partner in the law firm of Griffiths and Griffiths. For three years she was a member of the Michigan House of Representatives. In 1953 she was appointed judge in the Detroit Recorders Court. Ms. Griffiths was elected for the 17th Michigan District to the 84th through 93rd Congresses. During her terms she served on the Joint Economic Committee and was Chairman of the Subcommittee for Fiscal Policy. She was also a member of the Committee of Ways and Means.*

who propose a course of action that will promote the equality of women; to vote against those who do not support such equality. A woman voter, for a while at least, will need to let her party line count less, and the candidate's position on the rights of women more, than any other single issue.

Inequities in Financial Arrangements

At the present time a woman's dollar does not buy in the marketplace as much as a man's dollar buys. This is both illogical and unfair and it can be corrected by law.

A working couple, buying a home on a government-insured mortgage (F.H.A.) finds that only one-half of her salary will count toward determining the price of the home, unless she is a school teacher or a nurse—then all of her salary counts. This inequity occurs despite the fact that the government is guaranteeing the payment of the mortgage. A woman on a forty thousand dollars a year salary, maintaining her aged father who is drawing Social Security, finds that in order for her to purchase a fifty thousand dollar home, her father will have to be a co-signer with her for the mortgage. It seems curious that a seller would demand the signature of a man who could not possibly pay the mortgage. Are the lenders looking to him for payment, or are they merely perpetuating the myth that sales of homes should be made only to men? A married working woman finds that an insurance company will not sell her a policy to cover the payments on the home in case of her death, although they will sell her husband a policy to cover the payments in case of his death.

Why should a woman member of Congress pay more for medical insurance to cover herself and her husband than a male member of Congress pays to cover himself, his wife, and two small children? The reason cannot be that a woman member is more apt to be ill. The male member's policy also covers a woman and two small children. Nor can the answer be that a working woman is more apt to be ill than a working man. No questions are asked of the male member as to whether his wife is working. Why is it more difficult for a woman to obtain credit from a store than it is for a man? Credit, too, extends the value of the dollar.

The answer to these questions lies in the fact that a woman's income is thought to be temporary, terminating at her husband's whim or relocation. As a result of this perception of women's work, the dollars she earns do not give her the same purchasing power that a man's dollar gives him. The limitations on a woman's ability to obtain mortgage money is but one example. But it is an interesting case, since survey shows that a woman is more apt to pay for a home than a man. The purchase of life insurance is another instance in which women have had problems. Why should an insurance company refuse to sell what amounts to straight life insurance when a woman wishes to buy? It can hardly be argued that a woman is more apt to die than a man; life expectancy for women has been years higher than that of men for more than half a century. The marketplace, it is said, is a logical system. In the marketplace, only goods, money, and services are supposed to count—not sex, color, or religion.

It is true that new laws on credit passed by the Congress in 1975, as well as the new housing law, should correct some of these inequities. But all of them can and should be corrected by enforceable laws. Women's first demand of legislative bodies should be a guarantee that all dollars buy the same goods in the marketplace. Legislators who are unwilling to commit themselves to this proposition and to vote for it on every occasion should be defeated by women, regardless of their voting record on other issues.

Women and Taxes

A woman's tax money should insure her the same benefits in Social Security and the same rights to education at tax-supported institutions that a man's money buys. In addition, she should pay income tax at the same rate that a man pays. Yet the single woman or man pays from 17 to 20 percent more in income taxes on a given income than a married man pays, because the latter can split the income between himself and his wife. Yet, if his wife goes to work at a salary one-third lower than his, she does not pay a lower tax rate on her portion of the joint return. Her money is added to his and she starts paying taxes at the rate at which he finishes.

In addition, the working woman pays a Social Security payroll tax at the same rate as a man, although her husband cannot draw on her entitlement. If the husband is employed by the government and not covered by Social Security, he is not entitled to draw one-half of the amount of his wife's Social Security benefit.

But a wife can automatically draw on her husband's wage record, thereby increasing the couple's Social Security entitlement by one-third during the husband's lifetime. The wife can draw 100 percent of her husband's entitlement at his death, if she prefers that entitlement to her entitlement on her own earned income; but a husband cannot at his wife's death draw on her entitlement. Although a recent federal district court in Florida has held that the husband can draw on his wife's entitlement, it is too early to determine whether this ruling will stand.

Among the working couple in which both are covered by Social Security, the wife can draw her benefit or one-half of her husband's, whichever is greater. Why can she not draw both? She and her husband have paid taxes on thousands of additional dollars, as compared with the payments made by the man whose wife never worked. The explanation is certainly not based on need. If she had worked for the government and retired with a thirty thousand dollar pension, she would still be entitled to one-half of her husband's Social Security benefit.

Consider, also the Federal Inheritance Tax. The widow can inherit from her husband sixty thousand dollars tax free under any circumstances, if he has that amount to leave her. But at the death of a wife whose husband was the only worker outside the home (and if the wife brought nothing in inheritance or dower), the husband is not required to probate the estate. Everything belongs to him without any tax. Why should the wife but not the husband pay inheritance taxes? Working in the home would seem no less valuable than the husband's work. Moreover, if the husband had left his money to the church or any other charitable institution, the recipient would pay no tax.

Another aspect of sex discrimination via the tax system pertains to domestic servants. The wages paid to a domestic in the home are not deductible by the employer, perhaps because the domestic is not engaged in a profitmaking enterprise or because such a deduction would be a great boon to the rich. It would be a great boon to the worker, because it would encourage an increase in her wages, and to the middle-class woman who employs her because it would make her housekeeping dollar go farther. The true explanation for the fact that the wages of domestics are not deductible, I strongly suspect from long years on the tax committee of Congress, is that the committee has so little regard for the value of the work of a woman in the home. In the interest of equity, public policy should set a value on the work of a wife or on anyone who substitutes for her, through proper treatment in the tax laws.

Women need to protest such inequities in the law. They should demand that the inheritance tax code treat them as well as their husbands and they should communicate this determination to the Ways and Means Committee and the Finance Committee of Congress, as well as their own Congressman. The woman who remains single and works, who pays 17 to 20 percent more in federal income taxes than a married man with the same income, should also protest. The fact that the single man is similarly treated for federal income tax purpose hardly mitigates the inequity, since there are so many more women who are single.

Women and Unemployment

Two-thirds of all women in the labor force are either unmarried, divorced, widowed, separated, or have husbands who earn less than $7,000 a year. These women, by necessity, have a strong attachment to the labor force. They do not work for the "pin money," which is often assumed to motivate female employment of any sort. They cannot afford the approach of a dilettante, leaving or entering the workforce at whim. Yet when attitudes toward female unemployment are examined, it is clear that the myths of pin money, of marginal attachment, of random efforts to seek market work, are persistent and pervasive. It is male unemployment which is judged to be the important element of the unemployment scene. It is male unemployment which receives the vast majority of government assistance in training and job placement.

The Work Incentive, or WIN, program provides job training and employment services to recipients on the AFDC program (Aid to Families with Dependent Children). Almost all these families include a woman but only about a fifth include a man. However, when we look at the WIN program, designed to aid unemployed AFDC recipients, the incentive to work is extended 40 percent of the time to men—twice their representation as AFDC recipients—while women make up only 60 percent of the recipients of assistance under the WIN program. Moreover, although women's dropout rates from WIN are lower than men's, women are less likely to find job placement after completing training.

Why should women be given less incentive to work than men? Why should welfare be assumed to be the solution to problems of female poverty but work incentives be seen as the solution to male poverty? The answers to these questions appear to be that women are receiving treatment designed for a stereotype of female behavior which cannot be applied across the spectrum of situations women face today.

But unemployed women must deal with more than attitudes toward work incentives; they also have to deal with financial handicaps when unemployed. Pregnant women who are ready, willing, and able to work may be denied unemployment benefits automatically in some states. Many female state and local government employees are exluded from unemployment coverage. With lack of support during periods of unemployment, is it little wonder that many women decide that the costs of seeking work exceed the possible returns of finding a job?

Perhaps one of the most ominous warnings of future unemployment costs for women is the complacency associated with the acceptance of the higher rates of unemployment for women. Rather than attempting to reduce the sex difference in unemployment rates, many politicians and economists are rationalizing higher overall unemployment rates by suggesting that since women make up a larger proportion of unemployment than ever before, the unemployment situation may not be so critical. Surely women should not become the scapegoats for persistently high rates of unemployment.

Women and Educational Support

Women as well as men have traditionally paid taxes to support public schools; many of both sexes have also paid tuition to attend public universities. Men do not pay more tuition than women. Indeed, men are more apt to be the recipients of scholarships than women—athletic scholarships, or other state or federal paid scholarships.

Investigation has shown that for many years women were admitted by quota to most state institutions of higher education. Moreover, the percentage of women admitted to graduate schools, or to schools of law, medicine, or engineering has been very small. The woman applicant has often presented a better grade average for admission. Typically, she did well in the school, often holding positions of assistant to professors. Yet at graduation graduate schools frequently offer little help to young women who seek jobs. When hired, women have been given much lower salaries than men with fewer qualifications. Trained through a Ph.D. for a particular type of school administration post, one woman in her final year of training asked for advice on employment from the school. She was told by the head of the department that he had known only one woman who had ever held such a post, and that she was now dead. One is compelled to ask why the school took her money and her taxes to train her if they believed there would be no openings for women.

Title IX of the Civil Rights Act is now available to help young women in the field of education. It should be, and is being, used. Title VII of the same act, as well as the act decreeing equal pay for equal work, have been available since 1965 and 1964 respectively. They are now being used by women to open new doors to careers—careers that women have never had access to heretofore. The act has also been used to guarantee promotions and to equalize pay.

Legislative Needs

The possibility of giving the woman's dollar weight equal to the man's; of making her work earn in dollars what a man's comparable work earns; of improving her chances for education and employment in the field of her choice; of having her contribution as a housewife recognized by the government as a meaningful contribution with significant money value; of insuring that her taxes support not only the dependents of her male colleagues, but her own dependents as well—the potential for all these improvements have either been written into the law, or are under legislative consideration. But there are yet many long steps to take to guarantee equality of the sexes before the law.

In spite of all the laws that have been written to guarantee equality to women in the market place and in government, it is essential that the Equal Rights Amendment be ratified and placed in the Constitution. Laws can be rewritten. Court interpretations can be overturned. For the assurance of women generally, equal rights should be written into the Constitution. Once the Equal

Rights Amendment is passed, state legislators and United States' Congressmen will be compelled, when writing a law, to consider whether they have treated women equally. Should they fail to do so, any woman will have a right of action under the Constitution. Moreover, the Equal Rights Amendment would reduce the number of suits necessary to achieve equal rights for women. At the present time the courts are clogged with suits.

Even government enforcement of legislative and executive initiatives has bogged down, or been sporadic at best. In spite of major initiatives—the Civil Rights Act of 1964 (specifically, Title VII which created the Equal Employment Opportunity Commission), the Equal Pay Act of 1963, Executive Orders 11246 and 11375, and job training programs—the economic position of women has in many ways stagnated and even in some cases deteriorated.

Recent moves have improved the ability of government agencies to enforce these laws but there remain vast areas of discrimination yet to feel the pressure of either complaint or compliance. Legislation is only the first of several steps which must be taken before women and men have equal footing in American society.

The Possibilities for Tomorrow

When women have had access to the full range of educational opportunities, and when good jobs have been reasonably certain for a length of time, their attitudes toward careers versus marriage, or careers and marriage, may undergo a significant change. Even then, some women will continue to have special problems in pursuing careers. Women artists and writers are examples. Publishers cannot be made to print women's works, nor the public to buy the art works of women. Yet it is possible to insist that art institutes supported by public funds or tax deductible gifts give the works of women a fair chance, and that music groups supported by public funds or tax deductible gifts give women equal consideration. Similarly, programs aimed at sex equality will help women professionals in law, teaching, medicine, architecture, etc., although these programs cannot guarantee clients or patients. Women's performance in their studies and in their professional work should enable them to compete with men on equal terms. Such equality will eventually make it unnecessary for women to argue for special programs to redress the balance.

It should be unnecessary, for example, for women to seek help for day care. This demand emphasizes the degree of inequality between the sexes. Equality is achieved when women earn salaries that permit them to buy their own day care, as men do when faced with the need for such help. In fact, this is frequently the reason given for paying men more than women—they have children to support.

The woman who looks about her today, at the increasing divorce rates, at the abandoned wives and children, at the high number of women and children on welfare, at the high rate of inflation gnawing away at incomes and savings, is likely to realize that the most valuable gift she can bestow on her daughters is the gift of career opportunity. Once a career is established, however, today's woman faces most of the problems faced by the traditional woman, and some new ones. Should she give up her career for marriage? If her husband is given a promotion and a new territory, should she give up her own promising job, and accompany him, or should he turn down his offer? If the children are ill, who is to remain at home? Who has what responsibility for housework? In most instances, the wife has done as her husband wished. She has promoted his career and will continue to do so until a new value system shows both of them better and more satisfying lifestyles.

The years will not be easy. Equality between the sexes will not arrive instantly and it cannot be guaranteed by law. But it will come. And it will bring with it better marriages, a better family structure, and a far happier people.

Nancy Smith Barrett

8

The Economy Ahead of Us:

Will Women Have Different Roles?

The American economy in the second half of 1975 began a slow and difficult recovery from the worst recession in its postwar history. But even with the most optimistic assumptions about the fundamental soundness of American economic institutions, the wisdom of economic policymakers, the confidence of business managers, and the cooperation of working people, the return to prerecession rates of employment and capital utilization could be at least five years away.

Even if the economy could sustain a real growth rate of 6.5 percent per year for the remainder of the decade, unemployment would fall by only about 0.8 percent per year. With unemployment running a little below 9 percent in 1975, the rate five years hence would have slowly drifted down to 5 percent—an unemployment percentage still higher than the one in 1973, and substantially above what most people view as an acceptable "full-employment" rate of frictional or structural unemployment.

Figure 1 projects unemployment through 1980 under the assumption that real economic growth is sustained at an average rate of 6.5 percent each year. The gap between the actual labor

NANCY S. BARRETT *is presently on leave from the Chairmanship of the Department of Economics at American University and is Deputy Assistant Director for Fiscal Policy, Congressional Budget Office. Dr. Barrett has written books entitled* The Theory of Macroeconomic Policy *and* The Theory of Microeconomic Policy. *She has published numerous articles, primarily in the areas of economics, women, and unemployment.*

force and employment is unemployment. The difference between the potential and actual labor force represents "discouraged" workers who have dropped out of the labor force (or postponed entry) because they do not think they can find work. As employment increases, discouraged workers reenter the labor force in the hope of finding jobs, and these—together with normal increases due to population growth—swell the ranks of the unemployed. Consequently, for every ten new jobs created, perhaps four persons will enter the labor force, reducing unemployment by only 60 percent of the increase in employment. As shown in Figure 1, employment is likely to regain its prerecession level by 1977; but unemployment will not have fallen to its prerecession low of 4.6 percent until well into the 1980s.

Fig. 1. The Labor Force and Employment, 1973-1980

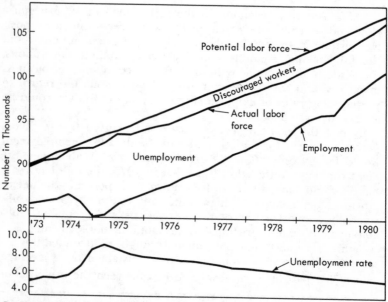

Sources: 1973:IV to 1975:II, U.S. Department of Labor, Bureau of Statistics; 1975:III to 1980:IV, based on various economic models.

Not since the Depression of the 1930s has there been a long period in which unemployment was so widespread. For half a decade or longer, many job seekers will be faced with closed doors; all will have fewer options than in the sixties and early seventies.

This job shortage is likely to affect not only people's labor market behavior, but also their attitudes.

During the period of economic expansion in the late 1960s and early 1970s, labor force participation of women, particularly of married women with children, increased dramatically. Participation rates for married women increased from around 30 percent in 1960 to 43 percent in 1974. Accompanying this trend was a growing concern with the issue of equality for women—equal access to high paying jobs and training, equal pay, and equal treatment under the law. Although there is little evidence that increasing female labor force participation in the sixties was accompanied by improvements in women's labor market status— the average job status of women relative to men actually declined during the period and the male-female earnings gap widened— there was, nevertheless a growing recognition that a problem existed. The women's movement grew in strength and influence, encouraged by gains made by earlier civil rights activists. Egalitarian attitudes became increasingly pervasive, particularly among young people.

A prolonged period of high unemployment could retard this progress. The recognition that jobs are scarce and are likely to remain so for a protracted period may result in a resurfacing of the view that secondary workers, notably women, should stay out of the job market, leaving the work to men with families to support. Despite the large and growing number of female-headed households, the notion that jobs should be apportioned on the basis of the male family head's need could shape attitudes about "women's place" in the economy of the 1980s.

This observation does not imply that the increased level of social consciousness on the issue of equality for women will necessarily be dissipated. However, the focus of egalitarian concern may well shift from the labor market to the household and to other nonmarket activities.

Alternatively, the recovery period could open up new labor market opportunities for women if increased effort is focused on preventing discrimination in hiring. As the economy recovers, employment will increase too, which means that new jobs will be available. Whether this occasions an improvement in the labor market status of women will depend very much on whether affirmative action and other policies to prevent discrimination are effective in countering the attitude that women should not be competing for jobs when unemployment is high. The reality of a large and growing number of female-headed households may also contribute to a more favorable view of women working.

Given these considerations, at the present time it is difficult to assess the longer-term impact of a high level of unemployment on women's labor market position. Women did not suffer as much as men from the initial impact of the recession. Employment of adult women held relatively steady through the downturn, while adult men experienced a decline of about 3 percent from peak to trough. Female unemployment increased 105 percent, as compared with 148 percent for males. The most severe cutbacks in employment were concentrated in manufacturing and contract construction—and in male strongholds within those sectors—while employment in services, government, domestic household work, and agriculture, areas in which women have a relatively large representation, actually increased. There is evidence that many women who would not have worked in ordinary times entered the labor force either because their husbands were out of work, or to supplement a sharply curtailed real income that resulted from inflation and a cutback in working hours. In many cases, it was easier for women to find jobs in clerical work, domestic service, etc., than for their husbands to find jobs in their traditional domain. Whether these women will continue to work when their husbands return to their jobs is uncertain. But a case could be made that they will be reluctant to give up the economic and social independence that market work affords.

As recovery proceeds, however, women could suffer from the job shortage, unless increased efforts to prevent discrimination are made in their behalf. Public employment programs and other transfers may be designed to exclude secondary workers with the rationalization that the "one-to-a-family" criterion will keep program expenditures low. Further, if high levels of unemployment continue, there will inevitably be more and more bumping of inexperienced and unskilled workers on the part of the skilled and potentially trainable. Given traditional attitudes regarding women's long-term labor force attachment (i.e., that they are intermittent workers), however unrealistic, the result could be a movement of men into previously female jobs, forcing many women to choose between being unemployed or dropping out of the labor force. It will not take the imagemakers long to reason that faced with this unhappy choice, a little stardust sprinkled on the home-and-hearth picture could be one way of inducing women to leave the work force. There is some question, however, whether such an approach would be effective with today's women workers.

Unlike previous postwar recessions, this one will leave in its wake an intensification of the fundamental structural imbalances that were present at its inception. Typically, recessions are viewed as a process of catharsis that somehow purify by adversity, weeding out inefficiency, weakening monopolistic influences, and encouraging flexible pricing patterns that facilitate structural readjustment. But in this case structural problems have only worsened as workers and machines have been idle. In the section which follows we will see how these factors foreshadow important changes for the American economy as it emerges from the recession in the next few years.

Background of the Current Recession

In order to appreciate the potential difficulties that will face the American economy in the 1980s, it is helpful to reflect on the events that precipitated the current recession. Strong excess demand pressures resulting from inadequate fiscal restraint during the Vietnam war engendered an inflationary psychology in American society that in turn induced a widespread fear of more inflation. This, in turn, introduced an anti-inflation bias into American public policy, a new development for Americans who had previously viewed unemployment as a far more serious threat. For the first time, people began reconsidering the so-called "inflation-unemployment" tradeoff and many came to the conclusion that unemployment, which affects a relatively small proportion of the labor force, is not too great a price to pay to prevent inflation, which affects almost everyone.

In the midst of this general fear of rising prices the United States economy suffered two huge inflationary shocks. Beginning in mid-1972, unfavorable worldwide weather conditions coupled with growing demand for food resulted in sky-rocketing food prices. Between December 1972 and December 1973 the food component of the Consumer Price Index rose over 20 percent. Following this, the cartel of oil-producing countries (OPEC) sent another inflationary jolt ripping through the world economy with actions that raised the price of foreign oil by about 400 percent per barrel, from $2.40 to about $10.00. The result was a 150 percent increase in the price of oil used by Americans.

One reaction of economic policymakers to these price increases took the form of imposing severe monetary and fiscal restraint. As inflation proceeded at double-digit rates, the nominal money supply was increased by only a few percent—not nearly enough to accomodate earlier levels of real spending. In real terms, the money supply actually declined by 9.4 percent from mid-1973 through the first quarter of 1975. With high rates of inflation, a progressive tax system produces nonlegislated tax increases. During 1973 and 1974, the effects of inflation alone produced a personal tax increase of over $9 billion. Nevertheless, attempts were made to reduce government spending; the President proposed a moratorium on new programs and undertook numerous actions to reduce expenditures for those remaining.

These deflationary actions came at a time when higher food and energy prices were eroding households' spending power. During 1974 wages failed to keep pace with inflation, and the dual effect of reduced real incomes and the threat of rising unemployment made consumers cautious in their spending. As a result of reductions in governmental and consumer outlays, business investment declined precipitously, and a deep recession developed. As output fell 7.8 percent, unemployment rose to 9.2 percent in May 1975, and capacity utilization fell to around 63 percent. In the first half of 1975 real GNP was only 86 percent of its potential, the lowest rate in the twenty-three years for which a measure of potential GNP is available (Figure 2). In current dollar terms, the GNP gap at mid-1975 was about $240 billion, more than $1,000 of lost output for every American. Although inflation started to level off during the first quarter of 1975, prices subsequently began to pick up again. These price increases mirrored higher food and energy prices and, to a lesser extent, the cost-of-living wage increases that accompanied them. It now appears likely that renewed inflation will reinforce the inflationary concerns that have characterized economic policy in the recession.

What does all this mean for the economy of the future? Clearly the inflation-unemployment situation is complicated by unanticipated shortages of key natural resources. When inflation occurs amid high unemployment and excess industrial capacity, traditional policy remedies do not offer unequivocal choices. However, it is important to recognize that what is done to solve current problems also affects future events. If the economy limps

Fig. 2. The "GNP GAP"

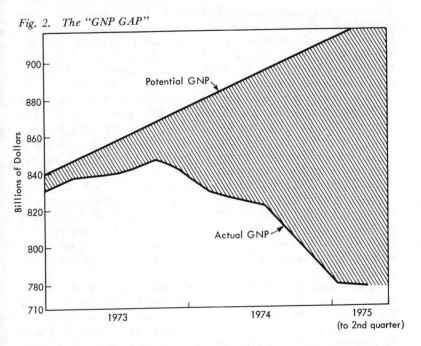

Sources: Potential GNP, Council of Economic Advisers; Actual GNP, Department of Commerce, Bureau of Economic Analysis.

along in semi-recession for the next five years, as many forecasters are projecting, the effect will be to dampen investment and capital growth. The skills of the unemployed will deteriorate. Ultimately, these factors will lead to lower productive capacity and slower growth in the future.

Consider an alternative scenario. Suppose the economy is able to expand rapidly (stimulated, perhaps, by a massive tax cut and substantial increases in the money supply), and energy and food prices are also allowed to rise. If the cost-of-living adjustments in wages were made through tax rebates to offset the increases in energy and food prices, the result would be an increase in the prices of energy and food relative to other goods. But such action would not need to produce a price-wage spiral such as would occur if compensation were made through cost-of-living adjustments to wages. As the economy recovers, there would be a shift in the composition of demand away from energy-using goods and services. The automobile industry would suffer, for instance, but there should be an increase in demand for mass transit. These shifts would hurt some industries and produce structural unemployment among specially trained workers, but they would also stimulate investment in other industries.

Such a policy would appear highly inflationary in the short run, since energy and food prices are included in measures of inflation. But it is not clear that the alternative—maintaining high unemployment in the face of rising energy and food prices—would be any less inflationary. In the longer run, the fast recovery option might be less damaging; to the extent that it encourages capital formation, puts people back to work quickly, and, as a consequence, is more conducive to long-run productivity growth, the second set of policies would seem to be preferable. The slow recovery option compounds the problem of increasing resource costs with low levels of capital accumulation and human capital development. This can only serve to intensify shortages in the 1980s.

Apart from being better for the economy, however, the fast recovery option should be considerably better for women as well. Significant moves toward equality in the marketplace during the 1960s and early 1970s could be continued before long periods of high unemployment threatened to wipe out much of the early gains. Attitudes that women do not "need" jobs as much as men—attitudes that, not surprisingly, disappear when labor is in short supply—are revived during periods of high unemployment to soften and rationalize the impact of last-in-first-out hiring practices. The faster new jobs are opening up, the less concern there will be about a job shortage; rapid recovery could provide many new labor market opportunities for women.

The fast recovery option would enable many women to continue to build up the seniority and work experience that would enable them to compete successfully in the labor market. By contrast, a slow recovery could have an impact on women's market work well into the 1980s if it forces a return to the allocation of jobs based on seniority and on-the-job training. Such a pattern of apportioning work opportunities would preclude women from competing with men in some occupations. Many women have invested heavily in education in order to enter new occupations; a resumption of the job potential of the 1960s would make it possible for such investments to bear important returns for both women and society in general.

The Economy of the 1980s

Turning to the somewhat longer run, there are again several possible scenarios for the economy of the 1980s; they turn in large part on how rapid a recovery from our current recession can be achieved. But whatever the outcome, there may well be some fundamental changes. If recession and slow growth continue to plague the economy through the remainder of this decade, we will enter the 1980s with a significant shortage of capital. There will be less physical equipment and the labor force will have fewer skills than full employment conditions would have produced. However, if economic policy reacts to the challenge of the energy crisis by taking measures to increase the production of other goods and services, there will necessarily be major shifts in demand away from energy-intensive items. In either case, unemployment is likely to be a major problem. Unemployment that occurs because of low levels of demand (demand-deficient unemployment) hits every segment of the population, but the unskilled, disadvantaged workers feel the pinch the hardest since the more able workers bump them out of jobs.

Jobs that provide training will be most scarce because of the abundance of pretrained workers to choose from and because training is an additional expense to the firm. New training will be available only to those workers with the greatest anticipated job attachment. Although women's attachment to the labor force has been increasing along with increases in their labor force participation rates, many employers continue to believe that women will drop out of the labor force to have children or for other family-related reasons. To the extent that jobs involving on-the-job training will be more limited in the next few years than in more prosperous times, the rationalization that women are intermittent workers will serve as a device for rationing such training. Women will likely have less access to training than they have had in the past. If this practice is tolerated the long-run consequence will be to increase the skill gap between men and women and hence to increase the gap in their future earning capacities.

Unemployment that occurs because of higher energy prices (structural unemployment) will be more concentrated in particular sectors. Transportation is likely to be especially hard hit. In this case skilled, blue-collar workers, predominantly males, may find it harder to get jobs than service workers. Since women represent over 50 percent of service workers they are likely to suffer less from energy-related unemployment than from recession-induced unemployment, assuming prevailing occupational patterns persist. However, to the extent that high unemployment, whether demand-deficient or structural, produces negative attitudes about women's labor force participation, both scenarios could result in a deterioration in the gains made by women in the tight labor markets of the 1960s.

Unemployment and Women Workers

In the American economy, periods of high unemployment have historically bred negative attitudes toward women working. When there are severe swings in economic activity, there arise social pressures for women and certain other groups of workers to move in and out of the labor force as the needs of the economy dictate. As the demand for labor grows in a boom period, these workers are encouraged to enter the labor force to prevent wages from rising too rapidly. In a recession, however, these people are not needed so a way must be found to ease them out.

Karl Marx observed that if society cannot find a mechanism to deal with this reserve army of unemployed, a social revolution is inevitable. In this perspective, the feminine mystique (a term used first by Betty Friedan to denote the multiplicity of society's attitudes about women's place, and their manifestations in the mass media and elsewhere) could be viewed as one mechanism for maintaining social stability in times of economic transition. The family-oriented housewife ideal that pervaded American society in the 1950s has sometimes been attributed to the return of men from the war and a desire for security and peace. But could another motive have been to get "Rosie the Riveter" out of the factory so that the returning men could find jobs? How willingly would the many women who joined the labor force during the Second World War have given up the independence, and satisfactions that went with earning a living without something better being held out as an alternative?

It is no accident that increasingly favorable attitudes toward women working accompanied the prosperity of the 1960s. Wages were rising fast, and, from the employer's perspective, women were usually willing to work for less than similarly qualified males. Despite the discussions of equality which surrounded the civil rights movement, women's wages relative to men's remained low during the 1960s and there was little, if any, improvement over the decade. Equal pay became mandatory for equal work, but women continued to be confined to lower-paying job categories. Women's wages average well below men's wages even after account has been taken of hours worked, experience, education, and age.

Now that unemployment seems destined to remain high for an extended period, the question of possible social unrest seems particularly pertinent. Unfortunately, the idea that the number of jobs is limited and must be apportioned to the most needy among the unemployed still surfaces in policy debates on public employment programs. If a government program "guarantees" everyone a job, some say, it should as a priority provide "one job to a family." Given prevailing attitudes, this means guaranteeing a job to the male member or else, among the very poor, encouraging the breakup of households. Labor unions too, concerned with seniority, are likely to be less interested in advancing women's rights than in the past. And the business community as well will have an interest in avoiding the social unrest that accompanies high unemployment.

Clearly, the most advantageous full-employment strategy would be to provide a job for everyone who wishes to work. But for the reasons outlined above, a return to full employment via this route is not likely in this decade. Another frequently voiced alternative is to reduce the number of job seekers, thereby artificially reducing the unemployment rate without increasing economic activity in the market economy.

Market Versus Nonmarket Work

Although high unemployment during the coming decade might well produce negative attitudes toward women's labor market activity, some features of a slower rate of economic growth could have a beneficial effect on women's role in society. Whether the economy stays in a depressed state throughout the decade as a result of the energy situation, or whether there is simply a shift in the composition of output, lifestyles may be expected to change. Less time spent in market work—either through a shorter workweek, more part-time work, or spells of unemployment—means that men and women will have more time to devote to leisure and to homework. Social, economic, and ecological pressures are likely to keep fertility rates low, even if women reduce their rates of labor force activity. The net result may be more shared household responsibilities, including child care, which is now the least shared of all housework, and thus more equality between men and women at home. As the economy recovers and labor becomes relatively scarce again, these changes should facilitate the transition of women out of the home and back into the labor force.

The line between work and leisure may become blurred as well. The person who stays home would not feel useless if he or she were contributing to fuel conservation and increasing the food supply. To the extent that nonmarket activity is felt to be socially useful, it is much more likely that nonworking people (predominantly women, given the prevailing patterns of behavior) will feel more content with staying out of the labor force than in the recent past. These same structural changes may also encourage men to participate more fully in family activity, producing a greater incidence of shared household and market responsibilities. Eventually, the increasing importance of nonmarket work may be conducive to new patterns of market versus nonmarket participation for both men and women.

WOMEN'S ECONOMIC INDEPENDENCE

When a woman engages in nonmarket activity the question of economic support immediately arises. In the current situation, a woman's desire to be financially independent is a major deterrent to her dropping out of or not entering the labor force. New feminist discussions may find it necessary to center their interest on financial support for nonmarket activities. Wages for housework, Social Security, private pensions, and other fringes for housewives will be matters of increased concern. Since nonmarket work is not included in the national accounts measure of Gross National Product, such payments would now be considered transfers. Some would argue that housework produces marketable goods and services and should be treated as market activity, but since these goods and services are not purchased (although they could be), it is difficult to put a price tag on them. It is noteworthy, however, that governmental output is included in the Gross

National Product, even though most public goods and services are not purchased. Wages paid for nonmarket work could be considered the value of the product, just as the wages of government employees are used as a measure of their output for purposes of the national accounts.

The question of who should pay the wages for nonmarket work is important. Should society bear the cost, or is it the responsibility of the market income earners in the family who consume the greater part of the woman's services? A large-scale governmental program to support housewives seems unlikely in the United States at present, although some other countries pay women child allowances on a routine basis. Contracts between family members are more likely, and perhaps more appropriate, although these represent a radical departure from established marital relationships. Attitudes toward marriage, toward the sanctity and unity of the family, militate against such practices. Yet the women's movement has done much to underscore the importance of financial independence for women. To the extent that society wishes to encourage women (or men) to spend less time in market work and more in home work, some solution will have to be found to provide the independence and economic security that now reside in a market job.

Governmental Response to the Changing Economic Environment

It seems likely in the 1980s there will be less confidence in the capacity of aggregate fiscal and monetary policy to cure the nation's inflation and unemployment ills; these remedies have been unable to insure a satisfactory level of employment and price stability during the 1970s. What is not clear, however, is the extent to which the government's programs to combat unemployment will concentrate on creating more jobs, or place more reliance on measures designed to reduce the size of the labor force.

PUBLIC EMPLOYMENT

One way to reduce unemployment is to create new jobs in the public sector; unfortunately, this is an expensive approach in the short run. A public service jobs program costing $5 billion would, at the most, create 600,000 jobs. Currently, 8.5 million people are officially unemployed, and another 1.5 million jobless who are no longer seeking work have been dropped from the un-employment rolls. To provide public service jobs for ten million people would involve an expenditure of over $80 billion, a sum that exceeds the current federal budget deficit. In the mid-seventies, the President and some members of Congress are op-posed to any measure that would increase the federal deficit. Consequently, it seems unlikely that public service employment will be an important counter-cyclical measure. To the extent that public jobs are provided, "one-to-a-family" restrictions may tend to favor male representation. In May 1975, 310,000 persons were in special public service jobs. Of these, 36 percent were women, although women made up 46 percent of the unemployed.

REDUCED WORKWEEK

Another way to reduce unemployment is to spread the avail-able work. The imposition of a significantly reduced workweek, as well as incentives to provide part-time work, would help to achieve this objective. These measures would favor female partic-ipation, since many women prefer jobs with fewer or more flexi-ble hours, and give men more free time, which could potentially increase male participation in family life. Some European countries, notably the Scandinavians, have been pushing media stereotypes of men in household roles. Such a campaign in this country opens a new range of possibilities for the advertising in-dustry. However, the high level of unemployment suggests that the emphasis may be more on family togetherness than on men assuming household responsibilities so their wives can work.

NEW GOVERNMENT SPENDING PROGRAMS

Changes in the composition of government services will also affect the demand for female labor. Even if little progress is made in the next decade in eliminating sex-role stereotypes in the marketplace, the huge volume of underutilized human and capital resources would seem to argue for the establishment of national priorities. If the argument is persuasive, the govern-ment's activities will be concerned with how resources are to be allocated in both the public and the private sector. For example, large-scale programs for the conservation of energy and other natural resources will create entirely new types of jobs. As was the case in the development of computer technology, women can make significant inroads in areas where new jobs are not sex-typed.

A second example of probable growth is the health field. This area, traditionally a female stronghold, will open up new opportunities for women as programs expand. Not only will expanded health services increase the number of jobs in traditional female fields as nursing and therapy, but increasing governmental influence over the medical profession could potentially eliminate practices which discriminate against women in medical schools and women physicians in hospitals. In countries with strict governmental regulation of medical education and hospitals, women have a much greater representation among physicians and hospital administrators than in this country.

CHILD CARE

It is not clear which direction social policy will take with respect to child care. As government assumes an increasing role in assuring minimal standards of health and welfare for all citizens—the aged, the disadvantaged, the jobless—attention is also likely to focus on the proper care for children. However, there may be a reluctance to facilitate increased labor force participation among women during a period of high unemployment; child care programs may be discouraged because they would increase women's potential for market work. There is evidence that some of the socialist countries actually use changes in the availability of places in day nurseries to control the female labor supply. Thus, while the government may assume an increased responsibility for the care of children of working mothers, it is possible that the facilities will not be designed so as to provide an inducement to women's labor force participation. In the development of day care there is likely to be a needs test and other restrictions on eligibility that will target the programs to the children of women who would be working in any case.

EQUAL EMPLOYMENT OPPORTUNITY LEGISLATION

Affirmative action and other legislation to prevent discrimination against women have been called into question as the economic situation has deteriorated. Uncertainty as to the degree of priority to be given to affirmative action is reflected in the debate over seniority versus affirmative action, and in continuing failure to enact the Equal Rights Amendment. The seniority issue is particulary important among blue-collar workers, and may become more critical if unemployment persists. Promotion to supervisory jobs is often based on seniority, and to give women equal representation often involves moving them over more senior persons, in violation of the established seniority system.

Concern over seniority inevitably becomes more intense as more people are laid off; consequently, affirmative action becomes more threatening in recession than in prosperity. In white-collar professional jobs, affirmative action poses difficulties associated with conceptions of "women's place." To the extent that social attitudes change as a result of the recession, hostility to the professional woman such as was encountered in the fifties and early sixties may reappear. Such hostility in the past has been accompanied by overtones of morality; women should be tending to their home responsibilities rather than taking men's jobs. Any recurrence of this attitude would make rational discussion of women's roles quite difficult.

On the other hand, economic recovery could provide new challenges for affirmative action. Layoffs will become less of a problem and firms will be taking on additional workers, albeit at a slow pace. Active pursuit of equal employment opportunity goals could ensure that women and other minorities receive their fair share of these jobs, not only in quantity, but also from a qualitative perspective. Although affirmative action may meet with more resistance when unemployment is high, there is no question that the opportunities for women are enhanced when employers are adding to their work forces in contrast to periods of declining or stationary employment.

OTHER MEASURES

Other measures to eliminate discrimination against women and to reduce their degree of inequality within the household have gained support in recent years. Equal treatment of women by the Social Security system and in private pension plans will continue to be debated, although there may be resistance to measures that would increase total Social Security benefits unless payroll taxes, too, are raised. It also seems unlikely that men's retirement benefits would be cut to bring women to equal status with no increase in total expenditures, in a period of declining real incomes. Individual as opposed to family taxation of personal income would also be a step in the direction of equal treatment of women, although such measures would be seen by some as an undesired incentive to increased female labor force participation, particularly among married women. Again egalitarian objectives might be construed as an impediment to the goal of reducing unemployment; this does not mean they are any less important, but only that the struggle for them will be more difficult.

Women in the Economy of the 1980s

The many structural changes ahead for the 1980s will pose new problems as well as new opportunities for women. Fear of inflation may produce policy responses that result in higher unemployment than occurred in the sixties, giving rise to negative attitudes toward women working. However, changes in the composition of demand should open up new roles for women, both in and out of the labor market. More part-time work may become available, facilitating flexible working schedules for women with small children. Increased emphasis on natural resource conservation and a slower rate of growth of real incomes may shift more focus to household activity for both men and women. Although home work may become more time consuming, it will be afforded a greater sense of social worth than in the earlier, more rapid growth period in which all status and worth came from the acquisition of material possessions and from labor market participation. Unlike the preindustrial era, however, fertility rates will be low. Consequently, there is likely to be equal sharing of *both* household tasks and market work among men and women.

All of these factors will affect women's perceptions of themselves and this, in turn, will shape the environment of which they are a part. The social and political power structure will undoubtedly remain in the marketplace. Women's chances of making inroads into the marketplace could be even lower than in the two preceding decades, depending largely on the demand for labor and the perceived attractiveness of nonmarket work relative to options in the marketplace. If the 1980s mark an important period of transition in lifestyles—a transition toward greater conservation, less emphasis on large families, more equitable sharing of home work—the gains to both sexes could nevertheless be more significant than those of earlier decades.

Index

The American Assembly
Columbia University

Trustees

Arthur G. Altschul	New York
Robert O. Anderson	New Mexico
George W. Ball	New York
Charles Benton	Illinois
William Block	Pennsylvania
Courtney C. Brown, *Chairman*	New York
William P. Bundy	New York
Bradley Currey, Jr.	Georgia
Robert H. Finch	California
Clifford M. Hardin	Missouri
Jerome H. Holland	New York
John Jay Iselin	New York
Sol M. Linowitz	District of Columbia
William J. McGill, *ex officio*	New York
Kathleen H. Mortimer	New York
Clifford C. Nelson, *President*	Connecticut
Chester W. Nimitz, Jr.	Connecticut
Isabel V. Sawhill	District of Columbia
Eleanor Bernert Sheldon	New York
Arthur R. Taylor	New York
Boris Yavitz, *ex officio*	New York

Trustees Emeriti

John Cowles	Minnesota
Marriner S. Eccles	Utah
Milton S. Eisenhower	Maryland
W. Averell Harriman	New York
J. Erik Jonsson	Texas
Henry M. Wriston	New York

About The American Assembly

The American Assembly was established by Dwight D. Eisenhower at Columbia University in 1950. It holds nonpartisan meetings and publishes authoritative books to illuminate issues of United States policy.

An affiliate of Columbia, with offices in the Graduate School of Business, the Assembly is a national educational institution incorporated in the State of New York.

The Assembly seeks to provide information, stimulate discussion, and evoke independent conclusions in matters of vital public interest.

AMERICAN ASSEMBLY SESSIONS

At least two national programs are initiated each year. Authorities are retained to write background papers presenting essential data and defining the main issues in each subject.

About sixty men and women representing a broad range of experience, competence, and American leadership meet for several days to discuss the Assembly topic and consider alternatives for national policy.

All Assemblies follow the same procedure. The background papers are sent to participants in advance of the Assembly. The Assembly meets in small groups for four or five lengthy periods. All groups use the same agenda. At the close of these informal sessions, participants adopt in plenary session a final report of findings and recommendations.

Regional, state, and local Assemblies are held following the national session at Arden House. Assemblies have also been held in England, Switzerland, Malaysia, Canada, the Caribbean, South America, Central America, the Philippines, and Japan. Over one hundred institutions have co-sponsored one or more Assemblies.

ARDEN HOUSE

Home of The American Assembly and scene of the national sessions is Arden House, which was given to Columbia University in 1950 by W. Averell Harriman. E. Roland Harriman joined his brother in contributing toward adaptation of the property for conference purposes. The buildings and surrounding land, known as the Harriman Campus of Columbia University, are fifty miles north of New York City.

Arden House is a distinguished conference center. It is self-supporting and operates throughout the year for use by organizations with educational objectives.

AMERICAN ASSEMBLY BOOKS

The background papers for each Assembly program are published in cloth and paperbound editions for use by individuals, libraries, businesses, public agencies, nongovernmental organizations, educational institutions, discussion and service groups. In this way the deliberations of Assembly sessions are continued and extended.

The subjects of Assembly programs to date are:
1951—United States-Western Europe Relationships
1952—Inflation
1953—Economic Security for Americans
1954—The United States' Stake in the United Nations
    —The Federal Government Service
1955—United States Agriculture
    —The Forty-Eight States
1956—The Representation of the United States Abroad
    —The United States and the Far East
1957—International Stability and Progress
    —Atoms for Power
1958—The United States and Africa
    —United States Monetary Policy
1959—Wages, Prices, Profits, and Productivity
    —The United States and Latin America
1960—The Federal Government and Higher Education
    —The Secretary of State
    —Goals for Americans
1961—Arms Control: Issues for the Public
    —Outer Space: Prospects for Man and Society
1962—Automation and Technological Change
    —Cultural Affairs and Foreign Relations
1963—The Population Dilemma
    —The United States and the Middle East
1964—The United States and Canada
    —The Congress and America's Future
1965—The Courts, the Public, and the Law Explosion
    —The United States and Japan
1966—State Legislatures in American Politics
    —A World of Nuclear Powers?
    —The United States and the Philippines